THE

CONTENTS.

MONMOUTHSHIRE.

Of Apparitions, &c. in England

A RELATION OF

APPARITIONS

OF

SPIRITS,

In the County of Monmouth,

AND THE PRINCIPALITY OF

W A L E S :

With other notable relations from England ; together
with observations about them, and instructions
from them : designed to confute and to
prevent the infidelity of denying
the being and Apparition
of Spirits ; which
Tends to Irreligion and Atheism.

By the late Rev. EDMUND JONES,
of the *Tranch.*

Nam Sadducæi quidem dicunt non esse resurrectionem
neque angelum, neque spiritum.----Acia xxiii. 8.

PREFACE.

THE Sequel, as the reader may see, contains very many notable relations of *Apparitions* and agencies of *Spirits*, both in Wales and England. And upon an honest review of the matter, I have no reason to question the truth of the substance of these relations. In such matters as these however it is easy to mistake in some of the circumstances of these relations, and scarce possible to escape them thro' the weakness of men's memories, and want of exquisite care to find out, and relate things as they are, where there is neither interest nor inclination to falsify the account of any thing. And I have this to say, as it appears in diverse places in the ensuing Treatise, that my conversation about these things was with religious persons, many of them Ministers of the Goespl, from whom I had these accounts ; which is the greatest argument that can be produced of the truth of these extraordinary and in some measure interesting truths, from which many things may be learned for the instruction in righteousness, and practice.

But some may yet enquire what may be the end and design of amassing together accounts of this nature, and making them publick? The design of all exercises of every sort is the chief circumstance that can belong to them, and therefore chiefly to be minded in all things.

In answer to this, I avow that it is designed to prevent a kind of Infidelity which seems to spread much in the kingdom, especially among the Gentry and Nobility, even the denial of the being of *Spirits* and *Apparitions*, which hath a tendency to irreligion

B

and atheism ; for when men come to deny the being of *Spirits*, the next step is to deny the being of God who is a *Spirit*, and the Father of *Spirits*. Some indeed will not deny the being of Spirits good and bad ; but without the least reason, or even a shadow of reason, deny their appearance. Who that reads the ensuing Treatise can deny the reality of *Apparitions* and *Spirits*? I really think none in their senses can. Also the Scripture of truth both the Old and New Testament speaks of the *Apparitions* of Spirit both good and bad ; and if they appeared in times past, why not in times present and future ? He must be a Deist and deny the word of God before he can deny *Apparitions* : our modern Deists are worse than the ancient Sadduces who owned the five books of Moses, though they owned no more ; but these deny the whole Scripture to their eternal destruction ; and those who deny the word of God, and make him a dumb God to his creatures, have no long way, or hard task, to deny his being.

And let us come to reason, (the Deist's God, which they put in the place of God's *Spirit* the guide to all truth ; and which they put in place of Scripture), is it reasonable to think that God who is a *Spirit* should create matter, as we see he hath done, even the whole material visible Creation, and not create *Spirits*, creatures of similarity to his own nature, which matter hath not ? It is against reason to think otherwise ; and having created *Spirits*, is it not unreasonable to think and say, that they never do, never should appear ? What sort of friends and servants should Angels be, and never appear to any of their friends and those they serve? And what sort of enemies, rulers and tempters, would the devils be, and yet never appear to those whom they rule, tempt, and trouble? I know *Spirits* are invisible without making use of some matter proper to their condition to appear in ; but who can say they never do this, and prove it? surely none can.

Let it be justly considered, that all the instances of *Apparitions* related in the sequel, are too great a sum of truth together to be reasonably denied, by the greatest infidel of them all; and what farther confirms this matter is that many authors have accidentally mentioned the *Apparitions* of *Spirits* in treating directly of other matters, and several authors of note and credit have directly wrote of these things; as GLANVIL, BAXTER, BURTON, MORTON, &c. And who can read SCHOFFER'S history of Lapland, MARTIN'S description of the Western Islands of Scotland, DUNCAN, CAMPBELL, &c. and question *Apparitions*? Also the complete history of Witchcraft, in 2 vols. 12mo. small Print, and very compendious; written by a nameless, but a very sound, judicious, and learned Author, exceeingly well read, both in ancient and modern history of Heathens and Christians, Papists and Protestants? He shews the numerous, various ways in which evil *Spirits* do appear and act, through Witches, Magicians, and Conjurors; and the accounts he gives agree with many of the accounts we have heard, and do hear from time to time. The histories he gives are very particular, and carry in them all the marks of authenticity: In the Preface he reasons very judiciously, both as a Philosopher and as a Divine; producing also the reasons of the most learned men who have written of this matter; as of KIRCHER, LE BRUN, --a learned Frenchman, and the famous Chancellor GERSON; and all he saith in a clear elegant stile: and in a word I think an incomparable writer on the subject.

If we consider farther that all which numerous authors of credit have written of *Apparitions*, is but a very small part of what have come to pass in the course of time, the argument still advances against

the sons of infidelity ; they are fools therefore who
think and speak against Scripture, constant experience, and reason.   And as the Author observes,
such men are too like the Heathen CELSUS and
LUCIAN, who would turn all things into fable,
illusion , and imposture.

There are but two sorts of beings, material beings
and *Spirits*.   And what reason can be given that
material beings only should be visible, but *Spirits*
never ?   When we have every necessary reason that
can be desired to believe that God himself, who is a
Spirit, took a visible human body, the master-piece
of the material creation, which was only fit for him
to take, that he might be seen working our salvation
and to be conversed with, 1 *Tim.* iii 16.   Great is
the mystry of Godliness, God hath appeared in the
flesh !   And the greatest argument for the *Apparition* of *Spirits* that can be produced ; for if the Crea-
tor of *Spirits* made himself visible in our world for
divers great ends, why should not the *Spirits* created
by him, make use of material things to appear by,
especially as they cannot always perform the works
they are either commanded or suffered to do in the
world, without appearing and making themselves
manifest one way or other ?   The ancient Egyptians,
Chaldeans, and Grecians, the wisest of the Heathens
believed the existence of *Spirits* and *Apparitions* ;
so the Old Testament Church, except the Sadduces,
who were therefore looked upon as heretics ; and the
inspired Apostle was against them, *Acts* xxiii. 6.
The arabians and the Persians speak much of the
Fairies ; and abundant facts, with arguments, are a
pregnant proof that should be received :   but if
people will be fools against reason and experience,
who can help them ?   They must be left to future
conviction of their unreasonable folly.

Rebuke to Infidels and Atheists.

—⁓⁓⁓—

TO those who ask of what use can the account of
the Agencies and Apparitions of Spirits be ?
My answer is, what real truth and kind of knowledge,
from heaven, earth, or hell, which cannot be made
useful to ingenious sober minds, who are willing to
make the best of every thing, which is the duty of
every man to do. And as to the account of Spirits
and Apparitions, it may be of these following uses,
and why not ? To prevent Sadduceism, and Atheism in some; to confirm others in the belief of Eternity and the World to come, and incline them the
more to a preparation for it. There are also many
things in the account, in this Treatise tending
strongly to prevent many evil practices, which do
trouble those are guilty of them in the world to
come, and to incline to the opposite practices of
good. Will any man be so foolish and irreligious as
to ask of what use can the Scripture accounts of
Spirits both in the Old and New Testaments be ? Is
Moses to be blamed for the account he gives of the
evil Spirit's deceiving our first parents, which caused
all the evils, the sins and miseries which have been in
the world ever since, and will be in the world, and
in hell for ever ? All the sins they do and the evils
they suffer ? Who, without any sense or reason, do
blame the account of Spirits ? The pagan world
lived in darkness for want of this account of the ruin
of mankind by a Spirit, related by Moses. Is the
Book of Samuel to be blamed for the accounts in it
of an evil Spirit appearing to the King of Israel, and
foretelling his destruction, and the destruction of
his sons and army ; and for saying that an evil Spirit

from the Lord troubled this King for his disobedi-
ence ?   Are the Books of 1st *Kings*, and 2 *Chron.*
to be blamed for the account given in them of an
evil Spirit deceiving four hundred Prophets to pro-
phesy lies in the name of the Lord, whereby the
King of Israel and two Armies were deceived to destruction, and King Jehosaphat brought to great
danger of his life ? Is the Prophet Zechariah to be
blamed for writing down to posterity that he saw
Satan in a vision standing at the right hand of
Joshua the High Priest to resist him ? *Zech.* iii. 1, 2.
Is the Evangelist Mathew to be blamed for writing
in the Gospel an account of an evil Spirit tempting
the Son of God ? And the other Evangelists' numerous accounts of Christ casting out Devils, and
of speeches between him and them ? Doth not the
Scripture plainly say that whatever is written in it
is for our instruction ? *Rom.* xv. 4. And therefore
the account of Spirits, every thing in it is profitable
for instruction, 2 *Tim.* iii. 16, 17. And above all,
the account of the first temptation in the beginning of
the Bible, which was the cause of all evils, and yet
the occasion of all good ; for it occasioned Christ's
coming from heaven to save----And the account of
Christ's temptation in the beginning of the Gospel,
Math. 4. and of Christ's victory, the ground of all
good. Besides all this, the knowledge of Spirits is
an interesting kind of knowledge which we are concerned to know, whether it be of good Spirits which
are our friends, or of evil Spirits, which are our
enemies ; for is it amiss for us to know our friends

and enemies ; Will any man of sense and consideration say it is amiss ?

How defective would the sacred Book of God,
the Bible be, without all the accounts of Spirits
contained in it ? especially those accounts of the
work of Spirits in the beginning of the Bible, and
of the New Testament ; to which all the great
things, both good and bad, in this world and the
next are one way or another related to, and con-
nected with.   It would be very odd that a spiritual
Book of this nature and size should be without
account of Spirits ;   cease therefore your idle
censures and   ridicule ye sons of Levity,   and
be sober and   considerate.

Vindication to the following Treatise.

THE Author's design in his account of the Agencies
and Apparitions of Spirits of the other world to
prevent the growth of Sadduceism, a great kind of infidelity, strongly and successfully tending to irreligion

and Atheism, being just and good; and at the same
time the relations abundantly proved from good honest
and virtuous persons, who had neither interest nor
inclination to tell a lye; being the most proper and
effectual way to prevent this dangerous hurtful kind of
infidelity: those persons are to be censured as weak,
unreasonable, and preverse, who will find fault with
this well-proved, and well-designed work; yet some
have been so week, inconsiderate, and unjust, as to
censure his account of Apparitions in the Parish of
Aberystruth; Persons neither capable of receiving reasons for it, or of giving any just reasons against it.
Nothing but perverseness and unreasonable confusion
and pertness, without respecting the Author's greater
age, knowledge, and experience, which puts me in
mind of the admirably profound Mr. Morgan Loyd's
saying----

" Pob gwaith da a gaiff ei groesi, ar ddyfnderoedd hoffant Boeri ;
" Maent yn cablu yr hyn ni welsant, ac yn llygru yr hyn y wyddant.'

ENGISHED---

" Every good thing will be crossed, and deep things will be despised ;
"Men blaspheme what they ha'nt seen & corrupt what they have known.'

Being of Spirits in the world, some infidels deny,
And therefore their appearance too they scornfully deny.

But the Scripture is not for them, against them is experience too,
Of all ages times and places, from the beginning until now.

Away therefore with their censure, against experience & the Scripture
Let them therefore be convinced of their error and ashamed.

Can evil Spirits be on earth and never yet appear,
And be always doing evil, not always can, its clear.

They are chiefly women, and men of weak woman-
ish understanding, who chiefly speak against the
account of Spirits and Apparitions, and others not so
ignorant do it for want of experience and consideration.
In some women it comes from a certain proud fineness,
excessive delicacy, and a superfine disposition, which
cannot bear to be disturbed with what is strange and
disagreeable to a pleasant vain mind : but why should
the daughters of mother Eve be so averse to hear of
the adversary Satan, with whom she first conversed
and whom she first believed, and was first deceived by
him ? with whom if they are saved they must com-
mence a warfare ; and are they fit to be soldiers who
know little or nothing of their enemies ? And so foolish
also as not to desire to know more of them in order to
be more able to contend with them ? Men of mascu-
line reasonable understandings and curious minds, are
not so unwilling to have a greater knowledge of the
other world to which all are going, even those who
shall go to heaven shall understand more of hell than
they did here, as Lazarus did in Abraham's bosom :
and where is the harm of obtaining a greater knowledge
of hell from the numerous and notable agencies and
Apparitions of Spirits related in this book ? especially
seeing we have many accounts of the Spirits of hell,
both in the Old and New Testament, recorded as
every thing else, for instruction in righteousness,
2 *Tim*. iii. 16 17. Let none therefore blame the wor-
thy Author's attempt : but if he has mis-related any
thing, he would be glad to be rectified ; for every
truth rightly related is precious in his own nature, and
may, and should be of some use.

C

*Enough is said in these relations to satisfy any rea-
sonable sober minded person, and to confute this ancient
Heresy, now much revived and spreading, especially
among the Gentry, and persons much enstranged from
God and spiritual things; and such as will not be
satisfied with things plainly proved and well-designed;
are, in this respect, no better than fools, and to be
despised as such.*

*------We think the Author able to answer all cavils,
and to be an overmatch for all the sons of Infidelity
in this particular.*

T. A.

I. A

H. R. P.

D. M.

VINDICATORS.

Tacitus prospicito omnia que quisque loquatur.--

——Disce, sed a Doctis.——

A RELATION OF

Numerous and Extraordinary

APPARITIONS OF SPIRITS,

Good and Bad,

IN THE PRINCIPALITY OF

WALES.

The Parish of Aberystruth.

A BOUT the latter end of the 16th century and the beginning of the 17th, there lived in the Valley of *Ebwy Fawr* one Walter John Harry, belonging to the people called the Quakers, a harmless honest man, and by occupation a Farrier; who went to live at *Ty yn y Fid*, in that Valley, where one Morgan Lewis, a Weaver, had lived before him, and after his death had appeared to some and troubled the house. One night Walter being in bed with his wife and awake, saw a light come up stairs, and expecting to see the spectre, and being somewhat afraid; though he was naturally a very fearless man, strove to awaken his wife by pinching her, but could not awake her; and seeing the spectre coming with a candle in his hand, and a white woolen cap upon his head, and the dress he always wore; resolved to speak to him, and did when he came near the bed, and said, " Morgan Lewis ! Why dost thou walk this earth ?" To which the Apparition gravely answered, like one in some distress, that it was because of some bottoms of wool which he had hid in the wall of the house, which he desired

C 2

him to take away, and then he would trouble them no more. And then Walter said, I charge thee Morgan Lewis in the name of God, that thou trouble my house no more ; at which, he vanished away and appeared no more.   He was no profane man, nor openly vicious. It is likely the poor man had in an hour of temptation unjustly concealed these things of some value, and was now troubled for it ; and chose that these bottoms of wool should be of use to others rather than be of no use ; though he neither requested they should be made use of, nor forbid their doing it, but left it to their choice.   No doubt but they made use them.

2. Long time after the death or removal of Walter John Harry, Thomas Miles Harry came to live at that house : who once coming home by night from Aberga- venny, his horse took fright on seeing something, (in- visible to Mr. Harry) and ran with him swiftly towards the house. Mr. H. being much terrified, hastened to unsaddle his horse, and on looking towards the other end of the yard, he perceived the appearance of a woman, so prodigiously tall as to be about half as high as the tall beech trees at the the other side of the yard ; and glad he was of a house to rest himself in.

3. Another time ---The same person coming home by night from a journey, when near *Ty yn y Llwyn*, saw the resemblance of fire, the west side of the river, onhis right hand; and looking towards the Mountain near the rock *Tarren y Trwyn*, on his left hand, all of a sudden, saw the fire near him on one side, and the appearance of a mastiff dog on the other side, at which he was exceedingly terrified.   The appearance of a mastiff dog was a most dreadful sight. He called at *Ty yn y Llwyn*, requesting the favour of a person to accompany him home ? The man of the house being acquainted with him, sent two of his servants with him home. ---My thoughts of Mr T. H. M. are, that he was a man of an affable disposition, innocent and harmless, and a respecter of what is good in his later days. His children also ; his son and two daughters were godly and religious. He was the grand-father

of that eminent and famous preacher of the Gospel Mr. THOMAS LEWIS, of *Lanharan*, in *Glamorganshire.*

4. His son Lewis Thomas, the father of Mr. Thos. Lewis, on his returning home from a journey, and, on passing through a field beyond *Pont Evan Lliwarch Bridge*, on the *Bedwellty* side of the river *Ebwy Fawr*, saw the dreadful resemblance of a man walking on his hands and feet and crossing the path just before him ; at which, his hair moved upon his head, his heart panted and beat violently, his flesh trembled, he felt not his clothes about him ; felt himself heavy and weak although a strong lively man. He remembered it all his days, and was very ready to declare it, having been much affected with it.

5. At one time two Gipsies came to his house when he was not at home, and seeing his wife by herself, began to be bold and very importunate for this and that which they wanted ; but she having an aversion for those kind of people, commanded them to be-gone, which they refused to do till she took down a stick and threatening to beat them, (being a strong couragious woman) at which, the Gipsies went away muttering and threatening revenge. Some night after they heard like a bowl rolling above stairs, from the upper end of the chamber to the middle of the room ---- stopping awhile----then rowling down to the foot of the stairs ; upon which, Lewis Thomas said to his wife "I believe the old Gipsy is come to give thee a visit." Next morning when she arose, she saw, on the floor, the print of a bare foot without a toe, ---dipped in soot ! and gone from the foot of the stair toward the door ! The next day when they went to churn, the cream soon began to froth as if it was turning to butter, but it did not though they churned it much ; they at length poured it into a vessel, where, after it had stayed some time, came a thick slimy cream above, and underneath it was water coloured with a little milk. They boiled the cream ---having a notion it would torment the Witch, and they were no more disturbed that way.

This was no Apparition, but the malicious trick of an old Witch in compact with the Devil. The

fashionable incredulity is to deny the being of
Witches. I am not certain whether they deny that
there ever were such persons in the world, or that
there are none at present. If they deny that there
ever were such things as Witches, the Scripture of
truth is against them.

Lewis Thomas Miles was a professor of some
note in the valley of *Ebwy Fawr*, and much
respected ; being an honest peaceable judicious man.
A good neighbour, husband, father, and an excellent companion ; though not absolutely free from
every kind of weakness----from which no man is free.
He entertained a meeting at his house, where the
ministers of *Penmain*, &c. preached : his wife also
being of that communion, to whom he gave no
trouble about baptism, nor to any one who came to
his house ; being of a very catholic spirit, though he
was in communion with the baptists and of that persuasion, as appears by what follows ; for he was
heard say that he prefered hearing the baptist preachers, because they preached the evangelic doctrines
truly, till they went to preach about baptism when
their subject did not lead to it, and when there was
no occasion for it, to hear one of them dappling
about it (so he expressed it) without bringing out
any thing clear about it, when he might have spoken
something else of greater benefit that was displeasing
to him. When he became old and infirm, he desired
leave of his brethren (the baptist church at *Tilery*) to
commune occasionally with the independents of
Penmain, who took the Lord's Supper at his house,
and they charitably gave him leave to do so.---I mention this to their honor, and that none may say that
all the baptists are rigid, though too many of them
give too much occasion to say so ; for here is not
only one particular person, but a whole baptist
church to prove the contrary : and it is right and
just to speak of the good that belongs to all persons
and things-- both in heaven and on earth. One can-

not speak amiss of any thing without being guilty of sin of some nature and degree or other; and worst of all to judge of good things and of great moment worse than they are; it is better to judge evil things to be worse than they are, though even that is also a sin.

It is ever to be observed, that the godly are the most moderate in all parties in religion, especially those who are the most humble and mortified to sin and the creature; some allowance to be made for particular tempers and dispositions, and provocations in displeasure; for oppression makes a wise man mad, *Eccle.* vii 7. But the hypocrites of all parties are usually rigid and censorious, as the pharisees who were hypocrites had the four leaven of unchari-tableness, *Luke* xii. 1 "Beware ye of the leaven of the Pharises, which is hypocrisy"; because hypo-crites are not sufficiently enlightened to see their sin and misery, and are therefore unhumbled, proud, and uncharitable.

JOHN AB JOHN, of *Coome Celin*, in the valley of the Church, was travelling very early in the morning, before day, towards *Caerleon* Fair, and, on going up hill on *Milvre Mountain*, he heard a shouting behind him as if it were on *Bryn Mawr*,--- which is part of the black mountain in Breconshire, and soon after heard the shouting at *Bwlch y Llwyn* on his left hand, nearer to him; upon which, he became oppressed with fear, and heavy in walking; and began to suspect it was no human but a diaboli-cal voice, designed to frighten him; having won-dered before what people could be shouting on the mountain so early in the morning. Being come up to the higher part of the mountain, he heard the shouting at *Gilvach* fields on the right---before him, which confirmed his fear: but, being past the *Gil-vach* fields, in the way to the cold springs, he heard

something coming behind him like the noise of
a coach; and what increased his fear the more,
was the voice of a woman with the coach which he
heard crying WOW UP. Now, as he knew that no
coach could go that way, and hearing the noise of a
coach approaching nearer and nearer, he was certain
it must be an evil Spirit following him; he was very
much terrified; and fearing he should see some horrid appearance, he walked a short distance from the
path and lay down with his face towards the heath,
fearing to look about until it had passed him : when
it was gone out of hearing---he arose ; and hearing
the birds singing as the day began to break, also seeing some sheep before him, his fear went quite off.

Here we may observe----That a christian may,
some time or other, have evils pursuing after him
and attending him on every hand; but while he goes
on in the way of his duty, they will not be suffered
to obscure his way, or but as he may either pass
over them, go through them, or pass by them on the
right or left, according to that blessed declaration of
the apostle, 1 *Cor.* x. 13. " There hath no temptation taken you but such as is common to man : but
God is faithful, who will not suffer you to be
tempted above that ye are able : but will, with the
temptation, make a way to escape, that ye may be
able to bear it".

Some readers will have a curiosity to know what
manner of man this person was, who had this remarkable trial in the course of his life. He was no
profane immorral man, but an honest peaceable
knowing man, and a very comely person ; and, in
his latter days after his conversation, he became
wholly mortified to this world, heavenly minded,
and died happy. More of him may be seen in the
geographical historical account of the Parish of
Aberystruth, printed in the year 1779.

W. E. of *Hafodafel,* going a journey upon the
Beacon Mountain, very early in the morning, passed
by the perfect likeness of a Coal Race, where really
there was none; there he saw many people very
busy;---some cutting the coal---some carrying it to
fill the sacks---some rising the loads upon the horses'
backs, &c.---This was an Agency of the Fairies
upon his visive faculty, and it was a wonderful extra
natural thing, and made a considerable impression
upon his mind. He was of undoubted veracity,---
a great man in the world,---and above telling an untruth. The power of Spirits, both good and bad,
is very great, not having the weight of bodies to
in-cumber and hinder their agility.

JOHN JENKINS, a poor man, who lived
near *Abertilery,* hanged himself in an hay-loft;
his sister presently after perceived him hanging, she
cried out with a loud voice ; upon which Jeremiah
James, who lived in Abertilery-House, looking
towards the place where John Jenkins lived, saw
the resemblance of a man coming from the hay-loft,
and violently turning upwards and downwards topsy-
turvy towards the river ; which was a dreadful sight
to a serious godly man, who saw the catastrophe,
and was very impressing; for it could be no other
but an evil Spirit going with his prey, the self-
murderer, to hell. Oh that men would beware of
Satan---the leader to hell, and not follow him to
eternal destruction, who delights in nothing but the
sin and misery of mankind. They that go more
softly in the way of sin, makes too much speed to
go to hell : but self murderers make the greatest
speed, and take the shortest way to hell. Some
follow after satan, but self-murderers go to meet
him.---They need not make such haste, for one hour
in hell will give them more than enough of it.---Oh
that this was more considered !

W. L. M. told me,---that going upon an errand by night, from the house of Jane Edmund, of *Abertilery*, he heard like the voice of many persons speaking one to the other, at some distance from him ; he again listened attentively, then he heard like the falling of a tree, which seemed to break other trees as it fell ; he then heard a weak voice--- like the voice of a person in pain and misery, which frightened him much, and prevented him proceeding on his journey. Those were Fairies which spoke in his hearing, and they doubtless spoke about his death, and imitated the moan which he made, when some time after he fell from off a tree, which proved his death. This account, previous to his death, he gave me himself. He was a man much alienated from the life of God, though surrounded with the means of knowledge and grace ; but there was no cause to question the veracity of his relation.

THE last Apparition of the Fairies in the Parish of *Aberystruth*, was in the the fields of the Widow of Mr. Edmund Miles, not long before her death --- Two men who were moving hay in one of her fields, the *Bedwellty* side of the river *Ebwy Fawr*, (one of whom is now an eminent man in his religious life) very early in the morning ; at which time they saw the chief Servant of the House coming through the field on the other side of the river, toward them, and like a marriage company of people with some bravery, in white aprons to meet him ; they met him and passed by, but of whom he seemed to them to take no notice. They asked the servant if he saw the marriage company ? he said "No", at the same time they could hardly think any marriage could come that way, and that time of the day. This certainly must have been Fairies, and was partly a pressage of Mrs. Miles's death, and partly it may be of the marriage of her daughter,---the heiress of the estate after the death of her brother Mr. John Miles, with that servant : the account of the Fairies, resembling a marriage company, could not be kept a secret from Mrs. Miles, which when she heard of it, gave her a deal of uneasiness, as she understood it as a pressage of her death, as indeed it was.

More of these kind of accounts may be seen in the geographical and historical account of the Parish of Aberystruth. If so many accounts of Apparitions have been found in one of the parishes in the county of Monmouth, how many may be found in all the Parishes in the County ? and how many in all the counties of Wales together ? Every reasonable person may easily see.

Is there nothing in all that hath been said already enough to stagger the unreasonable confidence of the sons of infidelity---the sadducees of these times ? And yet these are not all the accounts of Apparitions in Aberystruth Parish ; I have passed over several which would have been a farther confutation of this stubborn unreasonable infidelity. Every true instance of the appearance and agency of Spirits of the other world being a confutation of it ; and how much more so are many instances it really experienced and truly related.---Enough to make the deniers of Spirits and Apparitions great liars ; and if not to convince them in this world, enough to shame them hereafter. All men, sooner or later, will be made ashamed of their lies and errors : but better to be convinced now in time, than hereafter.

The Parish of Bedwellty.

From under the hand of the Rev. Mr. ROGER ROGERS, born and bred in this Parish, I have the following remarkable relation.---

A Very remarkable and odd sight was seen in July, 1760, acknowledged and confessed by several credible eye-witnesses of the same ; i. e. by

Lewis Thomas Jenkins's two daughters, virtuous
and good young women, (their father a good man
and a substantial freeholder) his manservant, his
maid-servant, Elizabeth David a neighbour and
tenant of the said Lewis Thomas, and Edmund
Roger a neighbour ; who were all making hayi n a
field called *Y Weirglod Fawr Dafolog* : the first
sight they saw was the resemblance of an innume-
rable flock of sheep, over a hill, called *Cefen
Rhychdir*, opposite the place where the spectators
stood, about a quarter of a mile distant from them :
soon after they saw them go up to a place called
Cefen Rhychdir ucha, about half-a-mile distant from
them, and then they went out of their sight, as if they
vanished in the air : about half-an-hour before sun-
set they all saw them again ; but all did not see them
in the same manner ; they saw them in different
forms.---Two of these persons saw them like sheep,
some saw them like grey-hounds, some like swine,
and some like naked infants : they appeared in the
shade of the mountain between them and the sun.
---The first sight was as if they rose up out of the
earth.---This was a notable appearance of the Fairies
seen by many credible witnesses. The sons of infidelity are very unreasonable not to believe the tes-
timonies of so many witnesses of the being of Spirits.

ABOUT the end of the 16 century, there lived
in the Valley of *Sirhowy*, in this Parish, David
Ziles, an honest substantial freeholder ; his house
was often troubled by night with Witches, who were
very mischievous, destroying the milk, &c. In pro-
cess of time, Hopkin David, a Quaker, by trade a
Turner, came there to work ; one night when he
was there, those Witches made a disturbance, which
he supposed was moving his tools ; he rose from
bed and went down stairs, there he saw them like
so many cats, and knowing what they were, spoke
to them, and asked one " Who art thou, and what

is thy name ?" to which she answered " Ellor-Sir-Gare",---(Carmarthenshire Elenor). He then asked another " Who art thou ?" the answer was " Mawd Anghyvion",---(Unrighteous Mawd) ; and the other answered "Isabel Anonest",---(Unjust Jesebel) ; to which he answered " Unjust is thy work in medling with my tools". He severely reproved and threatened them ; as they betrayed themselves and knew they were in danger of punishment, they did not trouble the house afterwards.---This good the honest Quaker did to an innocent honest family.

Had His Majesty King George the II. read the history of Witchcraft, and known as much as we do in some parts of Wales, he would not have called upon his parliament to determine that there are no such things as Witches, and his parliament would have hardly complimented him therin.---If they say there never was such things as Witches in the world, the Scripture is against them, both the Old and New Testament : for there were Witches in the days of Saul and in the days of Paul, or otherwise it would not have been written "O foolish Galations ; --who hath bewitched you that you should not obey the truth ? *Gal.* iii. 1   Yet His Majesty is, in some measure, to be excused, as there are not so many of those sort of people in Wales since the preaching of the Gospel hath prevailed in it. I know one woman in the Parish of Aberystruth who was supposed to be a Witch, and her son-in-law was possitive she was such ; though her daughter was a very good woman.

--- It is true this was no proper Apparition of Spirits, yet it was an Apparition of persons,---transformed by, and acting under the influence of evil Spirits, in the House of David Ziles, in the Valley of *Sirhowy.*

H. A. being a sheep stealer, and having stolen sheep from William David Richard, of *Rumney*, the said William David Richard, or some person employed by him went to a Dealer in the Black Art, who did something to H. A. which prevented him from seeing William David Richard's Sheep, though he could see other persons'. A very good punishment for a thief,---if it did not proceed from an evil cause.

JOHN JACOB, a Tailor, in this Parish, whom I knew, and was a man of sense and judgment, far from being fanciful and superstitious ;---as he was travelling one night, in the neighbourhood, lost his way. The Fairies, among whom he was now fallen, causing the ways to look strangely different from what they really were, found himself, all of a sudden, in a place where there was houses, shops, &c. as in a Town ; which, all of a sudden, vanished ; then he saw where he was, and came to a neighbour's house, he entered in and sat himself down very mute ; and being asked the reason of it, he declared what he had seen : he then began to look worse, and did not live long afterwards. We have little apprehension in our embodied state of the power of disembodied Spirits, until the all-shewing light of eternity opens upon us ;---which will amaze us with the new and great knowledge of things past and present.

E.T. travelling by night over *Bedwellty* Mountain, towards the Valley of *Ebwy Fawr*, where his house and estate was, within the Parish of *Aberystruth*, saw the Fairies on each side of him :---some dancing. He also heard the sound of a bugle horn, like persons hunting ; he then began to be afraid : but recollecting his having heard --- that if any person should happen to see any Fairies, if they draw out their knife they will vanish directly : he did so, and he saw them no more. This the old gentleman seriously related to me. He was a sober man, and of such strict veracity, that I heard him confess a truth against himself, when he was like to suffer loss for an imprudent step ; and though he was persuaded by some not to do it, yet he would persist in telling the truth, though it was to his own

hurt.---Such was the honesty of his nature ;---I mention it to obtain credit to the above relation--- to weak-
en the saduceistical infidelity ; for infidelity, some
times, and this among the rest, is very obstinate to
both reason and experience.

AT on time, on a watch-night, at the house of
Meridith Thomas, after the death of his child---about
four years old : the watch-nights then being very pro-
fanely kept in some parts of Wales ; the relations of the
dead were so silly as to suffer it, though it looked
like an insult upon their mourning and misery, and
had not the sense and courage to forbid it. Few
besides the dissenters did, but suffered it as a custom,
and because the pretence was to divert the relations of
the dead, and to lessen their sorrows : so improperly
and impiously turned the house of mourning into a
house of mirth, contrary to the Scripture declaration,
Eccl. vii. 2. "It is better to go to the house of
mourning than to go to the house of feasting ; for that
is the end of all men ; and the living will lay it to his
heart". But now the light of the Gospel hath prevailed against this madness. There came into the
house, at this time, some sober persons,---Margaret
Andrew, and William Harry Rees, both of the baptist
persuasion : there came also two profane men,---
Thomas Edward Morgan, and Anthony Aaron,---who
went to play at cards, and did swear most horridly :
but no one else would play with them.

While they were playing and swearing--- a lamentable
groaning noise was heard at the window, which surprised all, except the two men. William Harry Rees
persuaded them to leave off playing, and for some
time they did desist ; the groaning noise then ceased.
When the noise ceased they went playing again, (for
wicked men are commonly very incorrigible) and then
the lamentable groaning noise was renewed and was
louder. But when they were again desired to desist,
they said " it was only some person playing tricks to
try to frighten them" ; upon which William Harry Rees
told them it was no man ; but that the evil Spirit had

been a while by the house, and might come in and appear if they did not desist, and desired them to give over. Those hardy men yet would not venture out to see who it was playing tricks (as they called it). One of the company, being bolder than the rest, (for they all began to fear) said, " I will go and take the dogs with me, and see if there is any person about it". Accordingly he took the prime staff, and began to call the dogs to go with him : but the dogs would by no means go out, having likewise heard the groaning noise and feared : they sought to hide themselves under the stools, and about the people's feet. And though they beat them much, yet they would not go to door ; upon which William Harry Rees sharply told the two men to leave off playing, all the rest joining with him, for now they were fully convinced that there was an invisible agent near them. The two men at last left off playing, being convinced there was something extraordinary in it. The circumstance was made publickly known, and it had a good effect to prevent this wicked practice in that neighbourhood.

This was related to me by Elizabeth Isaac, an eye and ear witness of this extraordinary fact, a woman of careful veracity, and conscientious to tell the truth.

We have heard of other places where people played at cards until the Devil came among them, which hath much lessened the practice ; which yet alas much abounds in many places in this very sinful profane kingdom. Our parliament is busy seeking the welfare of this kingdom. It is to be wished they would extend their virtue against this wicked dangerous recreation. But alas, it doth not appear that they are careful to prevent sin and profaneness, which is the only thing that can prevent the ruin of this kingdom, whose welfare they continually seek, and study in another way ; though after all this, the only way to prevent it, is to prevent all manner of sin and profaneness, as far as it can be done. They do clearly see the misery of the kingdom, for it is great and they experience it, and justly lament it : but they do not sufficiently attend to the only cause of this---the great sinfulness in the kingdom. Should any great effect be consider'd, and the cause be wholly over-looked, without which the effect would not be, could not be. It is a wonder to some people, how so many wise and clear-sighted men in other things cannot see this. The Duke of Richmond did once, in the house of Lords, speak to this purpose,---that sin and profaneness was the cause of all our evils, and that the king should be addressed upon this head : but it seems he was not much minded, tho' nothing could be more properly and necessarily spoken. ---He was not seconded by the bishops who should be foremost in this work.

The Parish of Mynydduslwyn.

SOME years since, John the son of Watkin Elias Jones, a substantial man of this Parish, after his father's death, plowing in a field, when the Oxen rested, sent the lad which drove the Oxen to fetch something which he wanted, and before the lad came back, he saw a Cloud coming a-cross the field towards him, which came to him, and shadowed the Sun from him ; and out of the Cloud came a voice to him, which asked him, which of these three diseases he would chuse to die of,---The Fever, the Dropsy, or the Consumption, for one of them he must chuse in order to his end. He said he would rather die of the Consumption. He let the lad go home with the Oxen, and finding himself inclined to sleep he laid down and slept ; when he awoke he was indisposed, and fell by degrees into the Consumption whereof he died : yet lived more than a year after he had seen the Apparition in the Cloud, and heard the supernatural voice out of it. Some say, that he saw the similitude of a venerable old man in the Cloud speaking to him, and I believe it was so, and that it was the disembodied Spirit of some good man, likely one of his Ancestors, and not an Angel ; for Angels do not appear like old men, nor is it proper they should, because there is no decay in them as in men subject to mortality. It is not unreasonable

E

to think, that some times at least, the Spirits of
the Saints departed are ministering servants to the
heirs of Salvation as well as the Angels, and under
the name of Angels, seeing they have a nearer relation, and therefore an equal, if not superior propriety to do this. It is thought to be the Spirit of a
departed Saint who spoke to John, Rev. xix. 10.
" And I fell at his feet to worship him. And he
said unto me, See thou do it not : I am thy fellow-
servant, and of thy brethren, that have the testimony of Jesus. Worship God; for the testimony
of Jesus is the Spirit of prophecy." It would be odd
that the Angels should serve in the Church militant
upon earth who were never members of it, and that
none of those who have been members, and have
more experience of it should never serve in it.

He became very serious after this, tho' some times
a little fretful. He would often read and shed tears
in reading, and before his death gave good advise
to the family to be weaned from the world, to think
of the shortness of time, the certainty of death ; and
to prepare for eternity, &c. He did not tell of the
Apparition till within six weeks of his death. His
great Grandfather was an excellent minister, the
Rev, Mr. Watkin Jones, at *Penmain* ; several of
whose family was very religious. The promise is,
but too little minded and pleaded, that God sheweth
mercy to them that love him, to the third and fourth
generation.---What a sinful neglect and hurtful folly
it is to neglect this great and precious promise ;
which, if pleaded in faith and earnestness, would be
accomplished by him who hath said, " Ask, and it
shall be given you ; seek and ye shall find ; knock,
and it shall be opened unto you". *Mat*. vii. 7.

HERE is an account of a Spirit which came to the
house of Job John Harry, living at the *Trwyn* in
this Parish, and continued there from some time

before Christmas until Easter-Wednesday, which
was the last day of his abiding there : in which
space of time it spoke and did many things which
were very remarkable, as being done by an invisible
Spirit. The report of it spread very far, and is still
remembered and spoken of at times. Being aware
that some things might be added in the report, and
other things altered from what they really were, I
chuse not to relate all that I heard, but what I judge
most likely to be true. At first, it came knocking
at the door, chiefly by night, which it continued to
do for a length of time, by which they were often
deceived by opening it. At last it spoke to one who
opened the door, upon which they were much terrified, which being known, brought many of the
neighbours to watch with the family. T. E. foolishly brought a gun with him to shoot the Spirit, as
he said, and sat in the corner. As Job was coming
home that night from a journey, the Spirit met him
in the lane near the house, and told him that there
was a man come to the house to shoot him ; but he
said thou shall see how I will beat him. As soon as
Job was come to the house, Stones were thrown at
the man that brought the Gun, from which he re-
cieved severe blows : the company tried to defend
him from the blows of the Stones which did strike
him and no other person ; but it was in vain : so
that he was obliged to go home that night, though
it was very late,---he had a great way to go. When
this Spirit spoke, which was not very often, it was
mostly out of a Oven by the hearth's side. He
would sometimes in the night make some music
with Harry Job's Fiddle. One time it struck the
Cupboard with Stones, the marks of which were to
be seen, if they are not there still. Another time it
gave Job a gentle stroke upon his Toe when he was
going to bed ; upon which Job said, "Thou art curious in smiting", to which the Spirit answered, " I
can strike thee where I please". They were at

length grown fearless and bold to speak to it ; and
its speeches and actings were a recreation to them,
seeing it was a familiar kind of Spirit which did not
hurt them ; and informed them of some things which
they did not know.   An old man,   more bold than
wise, on hearing the Spirit just by him, threatened
to stick it with his knife, to which he received this
answer, "Thou fool, how can thou stick what
thou cannot see with thine eyes" ?   This Spirit told
them he came from *Pwll y Gasseg*,---(Mare's Pit) a
place so called in the adjacent mountain, and that
he knew them all before he came there.   One notable passage was thus, B. the wife of M. R. of L----l,
desired one of the family to ask the Spirit who it was
that killed W. R. the Scotchman : as soon as he
came home he did so, and the Spirit's answer was,
" Who bid thee ask that question" ?   to   which he
replied,   Blanch y Byd,---(Worldly Blanch) ; by
which name she was often   called afterwards, who
was a creditable substantial woman, of no evil qual-
lities, but that she was very industrious to gain the
world, though still in an honest way ;   she would
also do some charities.   Some of her posterity are
virtuous, creditable, substantial people.   On Easter
Wednesday he left the house, and said, Dos yn iach
Job,---(Farewell Job) to which Job said, "Where God
pleases".   Doubtless this was one of those sort of
Spirits which the Scriptures calls familiar Spirits,
and speaks much about them, warning the people
of Israel from seeking after them, *Levit*. xix. 31.
which intimates they would not have come to them
if they did not seek after them ; and therefore are
more in fault themselves than the Spirits :   Ordering the seekers after and the workers with familiar
Spirits to be stoned to death, and to be destroyed
from the land of the living, as not fit to be with
men on earth, but among the devils in hell.

This shews what a sin this was, which deserved an immature violent death. It is mentioned as one of the monstrous sins of Manasseh that he dealt with a familiar Spirit, 2 *Chron.* xxxiii. 6. It is said that the Lord slew Saul, the King of Israel, because he asked counsel of one that had a familiar Spirit, 1 *Chron.* x 13, 14. They are called familiar Spirits because they make some poor show of familiarity, and do some kind of services ; but their services are evil, and for evil ends.

This Spirit at the *Trewyn*, in *Mynydduslwyn*, was of this sort.---It never shewed any signs of virtue and goodness in any respect. It appears to me like a diabolished human Spirit, who had lived in sin and died in a state of enmity to God. I had once an opportunity to speak with David Job, whom I several times saw at the meeting at *Penmain*, who seemed to be a sober man : I asked him about the Agency of this Spirit which was at his father's house, he owned the substance of what was reported : he said that the cause of the Spirit coming there, was owing to his brother Harry making use of some Magic Spells,---yet without a design of bringing the Spirit there, but for some other idle purpose.

The Parish of Llanhyddel.

REES JOHN ROSSER, born at *Hen-dy* in this Parish, a very religious young man, on going very early in the morning to feed the Oxen, at a Barn called *Ysgybor y lann*, and having fed the Oxen, he lay himself upon the hay to rest ; while he lay there he heard like the sound of music coming near the Barn ; presently a large company came in the Barn with striped cloaths---some appeared more gay than others---and there danced at their music. He lay there as quiet as he could, thinking they would not see him, but in vain; for one of them, a woman, appearing better than the rest, brought him a striped cushion with four tassels, one at each corner of it, to put under his head. After some time the Cock crew at the house of *Blaen y Coome* hard by, upon which they appeared as if they were either surprised, or displeased; the cushion was then hastily taken from under his head, and they went away. The Spirits of darkness do not like the crowing of the Cock, because it gives notice of the approach of day; for they love darkness rather than light.---They surely belong to the kingdom of darkness, who hate and avoid the light of the sun; and if they are averse to the light of the natural sun, how much more so to the light of Christ, the Sun of the Spiritual world? And it hath been several times observed that these Fairies cannot endure to hear the name of God.---So far they are alienated from him, and become his enemies.

MARY M. living near *Crumlin* Bridge, and standing on the Bridge one evening, heard a weak voice like a person in distress going up the river, saying, O Duw beth y wnaf fi? O Duw beth y wnaf fi?---(O God what shall I do? O God what shall I do?) At first she thought it a human voice of one in distress; but while she was considering to think what the voice was like, a great terror seized her suddenly so that she thought her hair moved, and she could neither move forward or backward from the place where she stood; but seeing her cousin standing in the yard belonging to the house near the bridge, with great difficulty called her---who also had heard the lamentable voice, and came to her; when she came to the house she fainted: the voice which she heard was most probably the voice of some disembodied Spirit, who had lived---and died in sin, and felt the wrath of God for it; which

will make all impenitent sinners cry at last ! Our
Saviour saith, *Math*. xxv. 30. That hell is a place
of weeping and gnashing of teeth.---Oh that we
could prevail with men to to fear hell and damnation,
and the sin that leads to it.

LLANHYDDEL MOUNTAIN was former-
ly much talked of, and still remembered concerning
an Apparition which led many people astray both by
day and by night, upon this mountain. The Apparition was the resemblance of a poor old woman,
with an ablong four-cornered hat, ash-coloured
clothes, her apron thrown a-cross her shoulder, with
a pot or wooden Can in her hand, such as poor
people carry to fetch milk with, always going before them, sometimes crying out WOW UP. Who-
ever saw this Apparition, whether by night or in a
misty day, though well acquainted with the road,
they would be sure to lose their way ; for the road
appeared quite different to what it really was ; and so
far sometimes the fascination was, that they thought
they were going to their journey's end when they
were really going the contrary way. Sometimes they
heard her cry WOW UP, when they did not see her.
Sometimes, when they went out by night to fetch
coal, water, &c. they would hear the cry very near
them, and presently would hear it a-far off, as if it
was on the opposite Mountain, in the Parish of
Aberystruth, and sometimes passing by their ears.
The people have it by tradition, that it was the
Spirit of one Juan White, who lived time out of
mind in these parts, and was thought to be Witch ;
because the Mountain was not haunted with her
Apparition until after her death. When people
first lost their way, and saw her, they thought it
was a real woman which knew the way ; they were
glad to see her, and endeavoured to overtake her to
enquire about the way ; but they could never

over-take her, neither would she ever look back to see them; so that they never saw her face.

She has been seen and heard upon other Mountains, even as far up as the Black Mountain in Breconshire. Robert Williams, of *Langattock Crickhowel,* a substantial man and of undoubted veracity; as he was travelling one night over part of the Black Mountain, saw her; and having lost his way, called her to stay for him; but receiving no answer, thought she was deaf: he then hastened his pace, thinking to over-take her, but could not; for the swifter he ran the farther he was behind;---at which he wondered very much, neither did he know the reason of it, not thinking it was a Spirit which he saw and heard. In trying to over-take her his foot happened to slip in a marshy place, at which his vexation increased; he then heard her laugh at it, like an old woman: he was now much wearied and his mind greatly troubled, having some thoughts of an Apparition; and happening to draw out his knife for some purpose, she vanished: he then perceived he was in a most dangerous place; but he soon found his way home, and was very glad to find himself delivered from the unmerciful delusion.

She once led a man to and fro in a misty day at Pen y ddoi-gae Mountain; for after travelling much, he came to a bush of rushes; this gave him so great a concern, that he afterwards made a song of complaint and reproach against her, in which he mentioned her four-cornered hat, &c. but her chief haunt was on *Llanhyddel Mountain.*---I recollect hearing, when I was a young lad in Aberystruth Parish, of persons having lost their way in coming home from *Pont y Pool* Market, upon that Mountain.

I once met a woman of the next Parish, who, together with her young daughter, had lost her way in the day-time, and was very weary, especially the young lass, whom I put in the way. I lost the way myself two or three times, in the day-time, on this Mountain, though I knew it very well, and that is no more than a mile and a half long, and about half-a-mile broad

Once I lost my way,---as I came from the Mountain I called at a house where I had never been ; and finding an uncommon inclination to it, I offered to go to prayer, which they admitted, and I was greatly welcomed. I was then about twenty three years of age, and had begun to preach the everlasting Gospel. They seemed to admire that a person so young should be so warmly disposed ; few young men of my age being religious in this country then. Much good came into this house, and still continues in it. I think the Lord answered my earnest prayer, and if so the old hag got nothing by leading me astray that time. Often it is, that the malignity of evil Spirits is turned for good to them that fear God; and wonderful is the mercy that makes all things to work for good.---

Another time, on going over the Mountain on horseback, on a misty day, and thinking she might be near me, (for she was very busy on that Mountain observing who passed over it) I said in faith, "Do thy worst thou Old Devil, I will not loose my way" ; and I did not at that time.

Of late years there is but little talk about her, the light of the Gospel has driven her to closer quarters--- in the coal-pits and holes of the earth, until the day when she shall be gathered in the body to receive the everlasting curse, *Math.* xxv. 41. "Depart from me, ye cursed, into everlasting fire, prepared for the devil and his angels",

JENKIN JOHN DAVID was coming home one night from the Parish of *Aberytruth*, and in the way passed by the great Thorn Tree, upon the mountain between *Llanhyddel* and *Trevethen* Parish, not far from Blaen-nant dee fields, thinking to go over the mountain to *Blaen y Cnew*, about half a mile long. He travelled much ; at last the bridle unaccountably fell off the horse's head, he alighted to put it on, and looking where he was, saw that he was at the great Thorn, having rode his way backward,---He mounted his horse again, thinking he should not miss his way ; but after travelling much, the bridle again fell from the horse's head, and the horse would go no further, as if it apprehended its rider had lost his way : being tired, he alighted, and found he was again at the great Thorn. He then thought it was no use for him to attempt to cross the Mountain, so he went by the hedge side to *Ysgybor y Gruglwyn* Barn, under the eves of which he and his horse stayed the remainder part of the night, which was a long and tiresome night in the month of November. The before mentioned Thorn is there still, and must now be above a hundred years old. This is an instance of the longevity of the Thorn Tree,---the only one that I ever knew. The longevity of the Thorn Tree, of every tree, is worth notice, both in Divinity and Philosophy ; for the Scripture takes notice of it, *Isai*. lxv. 22. but the stupid world is careless and insensible of the works of God's power, wisdom and goodness, as it is complained of, *Isai*. v. 12.

Jenkin John David was the great grandfather of the late Rev. Mr. Herbert Jenkins of Maidstone, a dissenting Minister of every excellence of mind and disposition : Possessed also of every kind of ministerial gifts. Knowledge in the Scripture, memory, voice and utterance. &c. I am glad of this occasion to make an honourable mention of him.

THOMAS ANDREW, living at a place called the Farm, in this Parish, coming home by night, saw, by the side of a wall, the similitude of a dark man, creeping on all fours, scraping the ground, and looking aside one way and the other, also making a dreadful noise ; at which he was terribly frightened ; for it was, to every one that will seriously consider it, a dreadful appearance.

AS Thomas Andrew was coming towards home one night, with some persons with him, he heard,

as he thought, the sound of hunting : he was afraid
it was some person hunting the sheep, so he hastened on to meet and hinder them : he heard them coming towards him, though he saw them not : when
they came near him, their voices were but small,
but increasing as they went from him : they went
down the steep towards the River *Ebwy*, dividing
between this Parish and *Mynydduslwyn*, whereby
he knew that they were what are called *Cwn wybir*,
---(Sky Dogs) but in the inward part of Wales,
Cwn-annwn,---(Dogs of Hell). I have heard say
that these Spiritual Hunting Dogs have been heard
to pass by the eves of several houses before the
death of some one in the family. Thomas Andrew
was an honest religious man, who would not have
told an untruth either for fear or for favour.

The Parish of Bedwas.

MR HENRY LEWELIN, having been sent
by me to Samuel Davies, of *Ystrad Defodoc*
Parish, in Glamorganshire, to fetch a load of Books,
viz.---Bibles, Testaments, Watt's Psalms, Hymns,
and Songs for children, and coming home by night,
towards *Mynydduslwyn*, having just passed by
Clwyd yr Helygen* Ale-house, and being in dry
fair part of the lane, the Mare, which he rode,
stood still, and would go no farther, but drew
backward ; and presently he could see a living thing
round like a bowl, rolling from the right hand to the
left, crossing the lane, moving sometimes slow, and
sometimes very swift, swifter than a bird could fly,
though it had neither wings nor feet ; altering also

* Near *Clwyd yr Helygen*, in times past, and near the Place
where the Apparition was seen, the Lord's day was greatly profaned :
it may be also the adversary was angry at the good Books and the
Bringer of them ; for it knew what burden the Mare carried.

its size : it appeared three times, lesser one time than another ; it appeared least when near him, and seemed to roll towards the Mare's belly.---The Mare then would go forward, but he stopped her to see more carefully what it was. He stayed, as he thought, about three minutes, to look at it ; but fearing to see a worse sight, thought it time to speak to it, and said, " What seekest thou, thou foul thing ? In the Name of the Lord Jesus go away"; ---and by speaking this it vanished, as if it sunk in the ground near the Mare's feet. It appeared to be of a redish colour with a mixture of an ash colour.

I was glad to have this account from a strictly honest and a judicious man, perfectly free from enthusiasm and superstition ; especially as he had been in time past disputing with me against Apparitions. He did not deny the being of Spirits, but thought that men were deceived, and also told untruths about Apparitions. But going home from my house late at night, saw, going before him, the likeness of a large man ; and having come to it, it was a dark thing without regular members, and therefore forbore saying good night to him, whom before he thought to be a man ; he also, at that instance, remembered what he heard his father say,---that as he was travelling by night on a lonesome Mountain, he saw an ill-looking man, as he thought, coming to meet him ; he met him, and said, *Nos dawch,*--- (Good night to you) to which he received no answer, but was seized with terror ; upon which he said to himself, I was mistaken, no good night belongs to thee. Another time, as he was lying in bed in a chamber by himself, a strong pluck was given to the hair of his head, so that his head was sore for three or four days after. This he owned could be done by nothing but a Spirit.

I was glad that a person of his great excellences of mind and office was cured of this branch of

Infidelity. It is very improper that a Preacher of
the Gospel, and a Soldier against the kingdom of
Darkness, should deny the Agency and appearance
of the Spirits of Darkness being upon the earth.
Mr. Lewelin was a Preacher of the Gospel in Suf-
folk, in the dissenting way.

The Parish of Machen.

A S J W James was going towards *Bedwas*,
with a young woman, (whom he pretended to
court) towards *Risca*, and before they came opposite *Machen Hill*, they saw, on the east side of it,
facing the Parish of *Risca*, the resemblance of a
Boy, going before them : and while they were looking at it, they saw it put its head between its legs,
and transforming itself into a ball of Fire, rolling
towards the top of the Hill ; it being as easy for a
Spirit to go up as to come down. Presently after
they heard the jingling sound of Iron, with which
they saw many Horses drawing a load ; they went
beyond *Pont y Meister* Bridge, and then turned to
a cross lane leading towards a house where there
was a man laying dead : when they went a little
farther, they saw the earth cleaving and opening,
and out of it came a Pillar of Fire, which waving
in the air, singed the young woman's handkerchief
of a yellow colour, which could never be washed
out, but continued as long as any of the handkerchief
remained. The man afterwards seriously confessed
that it was his intention to debauch the young
woman in his journey, but this dreadful sight prevented his evil intention.

The Parish of Risca.

O NE W . J . a religious man, being sent to fetch
me to baptize his master's child, and upon
the way I heard him speak like a truly religious man,

and enquiring how he became under religious impres-
sions, he gave me the following extraordinary and
wonderful account :---

THAT he was once a Sabbath-breaker, at
Risca Village, where he frequently used to play
and visit the ale-houses on the Sabbath-day, and
there stay till late at night ; on returning homeward
he heard something walking behind him, and turning
to see what it was, he could see the likeness of a
man walking by his side ; he could not see his face,
and was afraid to look much at it, fearing it was an
evil Spirit, as it really was ; therefore he did not
wish it good night. This dreadful dangerous Apparition generally walked by the left side of him. It
afterwards appeared like a great Mastiff Dog,
which terrified him so much that he knew not where
he was : after it gone about half-a-mile, it
transformed itself into a great Fire, as large as a
small field, and resembled noise which the fire
makes in burning gorse. When he reached home,
he went to bed ; but he had dismal night of it,
fearing the evil Spirit was near him. It was sug-
gested to him that the devil would certainly come
and carry him away if he did not amend his life.
For some time he was very serious, and seemed fully
determined to reform himself from his usual habits ;
yet afterwards he seemed to continue vain and re-
gardless ; but not to break the Sabbath.---He was
much reformed by the preaching of the Gospel.

He related this to some young people, his com-
panions in vanity, who wanted to know the reason
of his change. They gave him the hearing, but
mended little or nothing ; so true is the saying from
heaven, *Luke* xvi. 30, 31. " If they hear not the
word, they will not hear, though one come from
the dead to warn them".---Here is an instance of it
in these young people, and in the young man himself,
---the relator of the extraordinary vision.

The Parish of Bassalleg.

THERE was a young woman called Anne William Frances, who, on going by night into a little grove of wood, near the house, heard pleasant music, and saw a company of Fairies dancing there: she took a pail of water there thinking it would gratify them. The next time she went there she had a shilling gave her, and so had for several nights after, until she had twenty one Shillings : her mother happening to find the money, questioned her where she had them, fearing she had stolen them; the girl would by no means tell until her mother went very severe upon her, threatening to beat her if she did not inform her how she came by it; she was then obliged to relate to her the circumstance, and they gave her no more money afterwards. I have heard of other places where people have had money from the Fairies, sometimes silver sixpences, but most commonly copper coin. As they cannot make money, it certainly must be money lost, or concealed by persons.

The Parish of St. Mellons.

IN the Parish of St. Mellons was heard the *Cyhirraeth*, (a doleful dreadful noise in the night before a burying) and coming the same way as the corpse was to come to church. Those that lived in the Village near the church, could not sleep well that night. One time a boy was sent to fetch a horse upon some occasion, heard it crying in the church : he first heard it in one place, then in another, and then in the third place where it rested. Some time after a corpse was brought to the church to be buried, but some person came and claimed the grave; they went to another place, and that was also claimed; they removed to a third place and

there had quiet ; just the same as the boy declared it.
Now it is plain that the boy told the truth of what he
had heard, for he knew not what was to come to pass ;
on the other hand---that this crying Spirit exactly
knew what would come to pass.   The knowledge of
Spirits, good and bad,   infinitely exceeds the knowledge of men upon earth.

The Town of Newport.

MRS. MORGAN, of *Newport*, told me there was
some persons drinking in a public-house ; two
of them officers of excise : one of them, to shew his
courage, said he would go to the Charnel and fetch a
Skull from thence, and did so ; they judged it might
be a woman's skull, though the grave nearly destroys
the difference between male and female before the
bones are turned into dust, and the difference then
quite destroyed and know only to God.   After they
had seen it he went with it back ; but in coming from
the church, a strong wind, like a whirlwind, blew
about him which brought with it a great terror, so
that he declared he would not do such a thing again
on any account.   His wife told Mrs. Morgan that his
cane, which hung in the room, beat against the wall
that same night dreadfully, and she was sure it was
done by some Spirit, and no accidental thing.

Here was a witness of the being of Spirits.---This
most certainly must have been the being of that Spirit
whose Skull was wantonly disturbed.

THERE was once a man who lived in my time, a
man greatly estranged from all good, and was thought
to use a dead man's skull to no good purpose, who
not long after fell sick, and was obliged to keep to his
bed. I heard that while he lay ill there was a man
appeared to him with a skull in his hand, which gave
him a violent blow upon his head, and made his nose

bleed. They heard the blow below stairs, which terrified them much. He died soon after.

The Parish of Lantarnam.

EDWARD FRANK, a young man, who lived in this Parish, went from home one day, and on his returning towards home by night, heard something walking towards him ; presently he perceived a large tall dismal object before him on the way. He was, with much difficulty, enabled to say, " In the name of God what is here ? Turn out of my way, or I will strike thee". It then disappeared. Soon after he was seized with the greatest terror, so that he knew not where he was ; he then saw, between him and the hedge, two dun coloured things like posts, which put him to the utmost terror, so that he could scarcely walk on, but seeing a cow not far off he went towards her to lean upon her ; she stood still, and suffered him to lean upon her. On going farther he called at a house, where there lived a young woman whom he was acquainted with ; he knocked at the door and asked admittance, but his voice being so weak she could not think who it could be ; she thinking it might be some person in distress, opened the door ; she then saw it was her well-known neighbour.---He being so much terrified was obliged to remain there that night. This circumstance was related to me by Abraham Lewelin, a religious person, who lodged in the same house with this young man.

The Parish of Pan-Teag.

MARGARET RICHARD, of this Parish, was with child by one Samuel Richard, who promised to marry her : the day being come which was appointed for the marriage, she went with two or three persons to *Pan-Teag* Church, where he was to have met her : they waited a long time, and seeing he

did not come, she fell on her knees and prayed to
God,---wishing he may not have rest in this world
nor in that which is come.   Soon after he was
taken ill and died; after his death he came to trouble her.   He never appeared by day, but always
between sun-setting and sun-rising.   She sometimes
saw him by her side ; she would then say to him,
What dost thou want ? or, Be quiet, let me alone.
Others saw him not, though she complained of his
haunting her; but they often saw signs of his being
with her ; whence she came to be called *Marged
yr Yspryd*,---(Spirit Margaret).   One notable sign
was this, which was seen several times, for having
brought the milk to the house, and finding herself
ready to faint, would hastily throw the pail of milk
on the table, and it would not spill, nor even move
in the pail, which was indeed miraculous.   It came
to be a practice with her to do this, which convinced all that saw it that it was the work of the Spirit
which haunted her.   One time she came to the
house of of Mr. Hercules Jenkins, at *Trosdra*, and
having stayed there till it was late in discourse with
Mrs. Jenkins about the Apparition, who asked her
to stay longer ; she answered, I must go now, or
else I shall be sure to meet with him in the way.
Mrs. Jenkins, a sober wise gentlewoman, advised
her to speak to him ; and tell him, thou dost forgive
him.   She went away, and as she was going towards
a stile at the end of a foot-bridge, she saw him at
the stile, waiting for her : she then asked him what
he wanted with her, to which he answered, I want
nothing, but do thou forgive me, and God will forgive thee.   Forgive me, and I shall be at rest, and
never trouble thee any more.   She forgave him,
and he shook hands with her in a friendly way, and
departed :   He never appeared to her any more.
Here is a lesson against fornication, and a warning
to people not to deal amiss with one another, in
this life, from the world of Spirits.

The Parish of Trefethin.

ANNE, the daughter of Mr. Herbert Jenkins, a young woman, well disposed to what is good, gave me the following relation :---

THAT as she was going one evening to milk the Cows by *Rhiw-newith*, and going through the wood under *Rhiw-neweth* to seek them, she saw something like a black man, standing by a holly-tree. She had a Bitch with her which saw it also, and ran towards him to bark at him, upon which it stretched out its black tongue, and the Bitch was frightened and ran back to the young woman turning about her feet for fear ; upon which the young woman was so terrified that she could scarcely speak : she found the Cows and brought them back to their own field, from whence they had strayed. And passing by the holly-tree back again, feared to look at it, lest she should see the same sight again ; but being past it, saw it again, very big in the middle and narrow at both ends, going before, treading very heavily, so that the ground seemed to tremble under it. It went towards a spring in that field which is under *Rhiw-newith*, called *Ffynnon yr Yspryd*,---(the Fountain of the Spirit) ; because of an Apparition formerly seen by it. About which it fetched a turn, and went over the stile from that field into the *Rhiw-newith*, the common way so called, and there he whistled so exceedingly strong, that the narrow Valley echoed it back, and then departed ; she then felt herself well.

This young woman's grandfather Wm. Jenkins, for some time kept a school at *Trefethin* Church, and coming home late in the evening, used to see the Fairies under an oak within two or three fields from the Church, between that and *Newynidd* Bridge. And one time he went to see the ground about the oak, and there was a reddish circle upon the grass, such as have been often seen under the female oak, called *Brenhin-bren,*----(King-Tree) wherein they danced. He was more apt to see them on Friday Evenings than any other day of the week. Some say, in this country, that Friday is apt to differ often from the rest of the week with respect to the weather ; that when the rest of the days of the week are fair, Friday is apt to be rainy, or cloudy ; and when the weather is foul, Friday is apt to be more fair. If there is any thing in it, I believe it must be with large and frequent exceptions, which yet may possibly consist with some measure of reality in the matter ; but of this I am no judge, having neglected to make observation of the matter. However, the prince of the power of darkness is called the prince of the power of the air, and doubtless not for nothing so called, *Eph.* ii. 2.

The Fairies dance in circles (which some writer, on the side of Infidelity unreasonably explain another way) in dry places ; and the scripture saith that the walk of evil Spirits is in dry places ; *Math.* xii. 44. chiefly under the Oak-tree, the female Oak especially, likely because of its more spreading branches, and of a greater shade under it. Perhaps also, and very probably, because of the superstitious, Idolatrous use made of it beyond other trees in the dark times of Paganism, which is an apostacy from God and true religion, in which the Spirits of darkness delight.

Formerly, in the days of ignorance, when men had but little knowledge and faith in God, it was dangerous to cut down a Female Oak in a fair dry place. Some were said to lose their lives for it, by a strange aching pain which admitted of no remedy, as one of my ancestors did ; but now that men have more knowledge and faith, this effect follows not.

A WOMAN born in the this Parish, who once was thought to be a virtuous and well disposed, but afterwards was alienated from God, and gave to the lust of the flesh.---After her death she appeared to her brother (a truly religious man) in his sleep, gave him a push on his breast to awaken him to more attention.   He knowing that she was dead, said to her, N. "What dost thou want here now" ? upon which she groaned and said nothing.   He then asked where she was, and how was it with her ; her answer was, that she was in a sore cold place, and that there was a sword over her head.   When he said to her, Give God praise ; much such a word as Joshua said to the malefactor Achan, *Josh.* vii. 19. "Give glory to the God of Israel", her answer was, no, I will not : and then departed.   Her brother thought he saw R. W. J. with her, with whom she had sinned against the Lord.

They are in a cold place indeed, who after death are sunk below the mercies of God, and the comfort of his mercies, where the warmth of his mercies never reaches.   When God's people here on earth are deserted, they are in the spiritual cold, and sorely complain of it, *Lam.* iii. 16. &c. And yet 'tis not so cold as in hell.   There is the eternal cold of discomfort, and the tormenting fire of God's wrath.   By the sword over her (woe and alas for it) nothing can be properly meant, but the impending sentence of the final curse, which shall be pronounced upon all the wicked in the great day of account, *Math.* xxv. 41. " Then shall he say also unto them on the left hand, Depart from me, ye cursed, into everlasting fire, prepared for the devil and his angels". Oh that people were afraid of this endless sad condition.

MANY years did the Spirit of Jenkin Parry appear unto several after his death, who had

given away his large estate from his relation : for a
warning to every person, beware of this kind of in-
justice, which gives so much trouble in the world
which is to come.

I WAS told once by an honest man, that Thos.
Cadogan of *Lanvihangel Lantarnam,* who had a
large Estate, nearly reaching from the mountain to
the river, and yet saw it not enough, but removed
his land-marks (being ignorant of the scripture
which forbids it, *Deut.* xix. 14, or disobedient to
it) farther off into the land of a widow woman,
which was yet worse, in order to enlarge his own,
which after his death was a trouble to him ; and
therefore appeared to a woman of the neighbourhood travelling by night, by a stile which she was to
pass over.   She, in a surprise, not recollecting
that he was dead, suddenly said, Mr. Cadogan,
what does you here this time of night ? to which he
answered, I was obliged to come, and desired her
to tell such a one to remove back the land-marks
which had been long injurious to the widow woman ;
and presently vanished away : upon which she recollected his death, and was much terrified.   And
well it was that it was kept out of her mind, like
Nebuchadnezzar's dream, for a time.   She declared
the Apparition and his request to the person he
named, and it was done as he desired.   He had no
son but three daughters to inherit his Estate ; but as
if the judgement of God followed the oppression,
they were ill married, and the Estate is gone
from the family.

Now if so many instances of the Apparition and
being of Spirits has been found in only thirteen
of the numerous Parishes of the County of *Monmouth,* how many more might there be found
in the rest of the County ? but however, I

shall proceed to give you an account of many
other remarkable relations of the Apparition and
being of Spirits in the rest of Counties in
the Principality of Wales.

Of Apparitions, &c. in the Isle and County of Anglesey.

I received the following account, which I hope is authentic, from a
young gentleman of *Anglesey,* concerning the Rev. Mr. HUGHES, a
Clergyman of the Church of England, who was counted the most
popular Preacher, and therefore the most followed in the County ;
and upon this account envied by the rest of the Clergy, which
occasioned his becoming a field Preacher for a time ; though he
was received into the Church again.

AT one time as he going by night to preach,
he came to a place where he saw an artificial
circle upon the ground between *Amlwch* Village
and St. *Elian* Church, which was said to be haunted by an evil Spirit. When he entered into the
circle, the similitude of a Greyhound came against
him, and he was presently pulled off his horse and
beaten. The next night, having occasion to go
that way, he went with an intention to speak to
the Spirit ; but when he came to the place he was
beaten again. He spoke to it, but received no
answer. Another time he passed by the place
without a horse, and he then saw that the Spirit
was chained ; he saw how far its chain reached, and
standing out of reach of its chain, he questioned the Spirit why he troubled those who passed by,
it spoke and said that as he was going with a company when he was alive to offer a silver groat (which
is expected and received at St. *Elian* Church) for
some Parish use, he had hid it under a stone, and
said he had lost it, to be excused from payment :
it told Mr. Hughes where it was, who found and

paid it, and the trouble ceased. There is something remarkable in the relation, but I deliver it as I had it from a person, who I am sure would not knowingly tell an untruth, or otherwise than as he had it.

In Carnarvonshire.

ABOUT the year 1758, at the house of a certain farmer, in the Parish of *Llanllechyd*, there was a great disturbance from an evil Spirit, casting stones into and about the house, beating and wounding the people. The stones were of different sizes up to 27 pound weight. Some Clergymen, from *Bangor*, came there to to read prayers, and they did their best with a good design, but they were also beaten and obliged to go away. Reading prayers was too weak a means to drive an enraged evil Spirit away. There was a necessity of some persons of a strong faith, who had the spirit and gift of prayer in some great measure. Most of the stones were river stones, taken out of the river which runs hard by. The disturbance was so great that the family was obliged to remove from thence. The person who related the story to the Rev. Mr. R. F. told him, he was struck with a stone of about five pound weight, as he thought.

In Denbighshire.

THE Rev. MR. THOMAS BADDY, who lived in *Denbigh* Town, and was a dissenting minister in that place, went into his study one night , and while he was reading or writing, he heard some one behind him laughing and grinning at him, which made him stop a little. It came again , and there he wrote on a piece of paper, that devil wounding scripture, *John* iii. " For this was the Son of God manifested, that he might destroy the works of the devil", and held it backwards towards him and the laughing ceased for ever ; for it was a melancholy word to a scoffing devil, and enough

to damp him.   It would have damped him yet more, if
he had shewn him   *Jam.* ii. 19,   " The devils believe
and tremble".   But he had enough for one time.

MR. BADDY was the grandfather of the late Rev.
Mr. David Jordine, who was the Tutor of the Ortho-
dox Academy, at *Abergavenny,* who told me of the
before-mentioned passage concerning his grandfather.

I AM now going to relate one of the most extraordinary Apparitions that ever was communicated to me,
either by word of mouth,   or by letter ;   which I received from the hand of a pious young gentleman of
Denbighshire then at school, who was an eye witness
of it, as follows :---

MARCH, 24th, 1772.

Rev. SIR,

   Concerning the Apparition *I saw, I
shall relate it as well as I can in all its particulars.
As far as I can remember it was in the year 1757,
in a summer's day,   about noon,   I, with three others,
one of which was a sister of mine, and the other two
were sisters.   We were playing in a field called*
Kae-kaled,   *in the Parish of* Bodvary, *in the County
of* Denbigh, *near the stile which is next* Lanelwyd
house, *where we perceived a company of dancers, in
the middle of the field, about seventy yards from us.
We could not tell their numbers, because of the swiftness
of their motions, which seemed to be after the manner of*
Morris-dancers, *(something uncommonly wild in their
motions) but after looking some time we came to guess
that their number might be about fifteen or sixteen.
They were clothed in red like soldiers, with red hand-
kerchiefs spotted with yellow about their heads.   They*

H

*seemed to be a little bigger than we, but of a dwarfish
appearance. Upon this we reasoned together what they
might be, whence they came, and what they were about.
Presently we saw one of them coming away from the
company in a running pace ; upon seeing this we began
to be afraid and ran to the stile.* BARBARA JONES
*went over the stile first, next her sister, next to that my
sister, and last of all myself : while I was creeping up
the stile, my sister staying to help me, I looked back
and saw him just by me ; upon which I cried out, my
sister also cried out, and took hold of me under her
arm to draw me over ; and when my feet had just come
over, I still crying and looking back, we saw him
reaching after me, leaning on the stile ; but did not
come over. Away we ran towards the house, called the
people out, and went trembling towards the place ;
which might be about one hundred and fifty yards of
the house : but though we came so soon to see, yet we
could see nothing of them. He who came near us had
a grim countenance, a wild, and somewhat fierce look.
He came towards us in a slow running pace, but with
long steps for a little one. His complexion was copper-
coloured, which might be significative of his disposition
and condition ; for they were not good, but therefore
bad* Spirits. *The red---of their cruelty ; The black---
of their sin and misery ; and he looked rather old
than young.*

    The dress, the form, the colour, and the size
Of these, dear Sir, did me surprise ;
The open view of them we had four,
Their sudden flight and seeing them no more, }
Do still confirm the wonder more and more.)

                 Thus far Mr. E. W--------'s *Letter.*

THE oddish appearance of the Spectre brings to my mind an Apparition seen in this Parish of *Trefethin*, which for brevity sake I passed over there, and comes properly to be mentioned here as follows :---

P. W. who lived at the SHIP in *Pont y Pool*, and born also in *Trefethin* Parish :---An honest virtuous woman, when a young girl going to school, one time seeing the Fairies dancing in a pleasant dry place under a crab tree, and seeing them like children much of her own size, and hearing a small pleasant music among them, went to them, and was induced to dance with them ; and she brought them unto an empty barn to dance.   This she did at times both going and coming from school for three or four years.   Though she danced so often with them, yet she could never hear the sound of their feet ; therefore she took off her shoes that she might not make a noise with her feet, which thought was displeasing unto them.   Some in the house observing her without shoes, said, this girl walks without shoes to school : but she did not tell them of her adventure with the Fairies.   They all blue and green aprons on : they were of a small stature, and appeared rather old.

All the Spirits of hell cannot make as good appearance, and divert themselves in the hellish state, as the Fairies do, who are nothing else, after all the talking about them, but the disembodied Spirits of men, who lived and died without the enjoyment of the means of grace and salvation, as Pagans and others, and their condemnation therefore far less than those who have enjoyed the means of salvation, *Math.* xi. 20, to 24. The condemnation of men will be according to the light and means of grace they have enjoyed and abused ; according to the words of the Apostle, *Rom.* ii. 12, to 16.   When she gave over going with them to dance, they shewed their displeasure ; and because they could not prevail, did hurt her, by dislocating one of her walking members, which was afterwards put in place.   Here is one instance of their malignity, and shews to whom they belong.

H 2

In Merionithshire.

IN the year 1694, there was a strange fire which kindled in the night about Harlech-Town, in this County, chiefly in the night time, and continued for several months, but chiefly active in two months. It was a weak blue flame, which burned little else but corn and ricks of hay, and the thatch of houses. Every night there was a hue and cry that such a house, hay, or corn was burning, and the neighbours ran together to extinguish it ; and as it was not a very strong fire, they ran into it to extinguish it ; though they must not stay long in it. Some, most of the learned, called it a Meteor, which came from the sea on the the *Carnarvon* side. But if a Meteor from the *Carnarvon* side, why not rather in *Carnarvon* than *Merionithshire* ? why in *Merionithshire* than any other part of WALES, or in the world ? why no where else in the County but about *Harlech* ? And why at that time more than before or after ? The people gave another account of it in former days ;---that it was an effect of witchcraft, which is the more likely thing, as it cannot be accounted from nature.

In Montgomeryshire.

EDWARD LLOYD, in the Parish of *Langyrig*, being very ill ; those that were with him heard the voice of some person very near them; they looked about the house, but could see no person, the voice seemed to be in the room were they were. Soon after they heard these words, by something unseen, *Y mae Nenbren y Ty yn craccio,*---(the uppermost beam of the house cracketh) ; soon after, *Fe dorr yn y man,*---(it will presently break) ; then they heard the same voice say, *Dyna fy yn torri,*---(there it breaks) ; he died that moment, which much affected the company.

In Radnorshire.

I N *Llynwent,* a place so called in this Country, where an old chapel had been built, but now turned to secular use. At a certain time when the man of the house and his wife were gone from home : while the rest of the family were at supper, three of the servants heard the sound of horses coming towards the house, and thinking their master and mistress were coming, said, there they are coming, and went out to meet them, but saw nothing ; they wondered at it, and the rest laughing at them. They sat at the fire, and heard as it were the sound of people passing by them and going up stairs, and talking among themselves, which they telling, the others at the table laughing at them, though herein their levity too apt to be on such occasions was wrong; for behold not long after three of the family fell sick and died.

IN the house of Edward Roberts, in the Parish of *Llangynllo,* came to pass a stranger thing.--- As the servant-man was threshing, the threshel was taken out of his hand and thrown upon the hay-loft ; he minded it not much : but being taken out of his hand three of four times gave him a concern, and he went to the house and told it. Edward Roberts being from home, his wife and the maid made light of it, and merrily said they would come with him to keep him from the Spirit, and went there ; the one to knit, and the other to wind yarn. They were not long there before what they brought there were taken out of their hands, and tumbled about in their sight ; on seeing this, they shut the barn door and came away more sober than they went there. They had not been long home before they perceived the dishes on the shelf move backwards, and some were thrown down : most of the earthen vessels

were broke, especially in the night ; for in the
morning they could scarce tread without stepping
upon wrecks of something which lay on the ground.
This circumstance being made known, induced the
neighbours to visit them.   Some came from far to
satisfy their curiosity ; some from *Knighton* ; and
one came from thence to read, confident he would
silence the evil Spirit ; but had the book taken out
of his hand and thrown up stairs.   There were
stones cast among them, and were often struck by
them, but they were not much hurt : there was also
iron thrown from the chimney at them, and they
knew not from whence it came.   The stir continued
there about a quarter of a year.   At last the house
took fire, which they attempted to quench ; but it
was in vain.   They saved most of the furniture, but
the house was burnt to the ground ;   so that nothing
but the walls, and the two chimneys, stood as a
public spectacle to those who passed to and
from *Knighton*   Market.

The apparent cause of the disturbance was this,---
Griffith Meridith and his wife, the   father and
mother of Edward Roberts's wife were dead, and
their son, who was heir to the house, enlisted
himself a soldier, and left the country.   Roberts
and his wife, who were Tenants in the house that
was burnt, removed into their father's house ; he
being dead, and the house much decayed, they repaired it, and claimed it, as thinking it was their
own, and that her brother would never return : but
in that year the brother unexpectedly came home,
thinking to see his father ; he wondered to see the
house altered, and making enquiry, went to his
sister and claimed the house ; which she refused, as
having been at charge with it.   At last he desired
only a share of it, which she also refused ; he then
desired but two guineas for it, which she still re-
fusing ; he went away for *Ireland*, threatening his

sister that she should repent for this ill dealing ; and she had cause to repent.

Now here was very plainly the work of some Spirit, enough to convince, or at least confound an Atheist of the being of Spirits ; but whether it was her brother's own Spirit after his death, or an evil Spirit which he employed to work this revenge upon an unnatural sister, cannot be determined, but the last is more likely.

In Brecknockshire.

WALTER WATKINS, of the *Neuath*, in the Parish of *Landdetty*, a man of virtue, sense, and learning, gave me the following notable relation of an Apparition, as follows :---

That on going one night towards *Tafe Fechan* Chapel, not far from his house, he saw a light near the said Chapel ; it increased till it was as big as a Church Tower, and decreased again until it became as small as a star, and then it would increase to the former largeness, doing so several times ; at which he wondered very much, but felt no fear. He went to the house to fetch his father and mother to see it, and they all saw it in the same manner, to their great astonishment. Sometime after as a neighbour was ploughing a field, near the Chapel, the plough stopped against a large flat stone, which the ploughers rose up, and behold there was a stone chest, and in it was the jaw-bone of a man, and an empty earthen jug ; it was supposed to have been some person murdered, but by whom it could not be known ; but shall be known in eternity. However, upon this discovery, it was remembered by some, that a man named Philip Watkins, living at the said *Neuath*, was suddenly lost and never heard of after.

His wife married again, thinking he certainly must be dead, or pretending to think so.

Some time after this woman asking a wandering sort of man, who used to be between the two houses, what news from *Neuath* ? he jocosely said, Philip Watkins was come home, and was well. This affected her so much that she fell sick and died. It was in vain for the man to say afterwards that it was not true, and that he only jested. If she was sorry for having married again, it shewed a tender conscience ; otherwise it looked like extreme guilt : there is a mystery in it which must be left undecided this side of eternity, which all things which have been done on earth shall be known ; according to our Saviour's saying, *Luke* xii. 2. " For there is nothing covered that shall not be revealed, neither hid that shall not be known ; in the day when the secrets of men shall be revealed".

After this the light was no more seen near the Chapel, though often seen before. The Spirits of men appear like light, because they are knowing beings, properly resembled by light.

———

I N the Parish of *Ystrad-gynlas*, in the same County, came to pass the following remakable occurrence, which I had from under the hand of the Rev. Mr. T. L. who then lived in that neighbourhood :

A young man, son to an inn-keeper, being often troubled by supernatural odd sights ; at last a Spirit appeared to him in the shape of a well dressed woman, who stood before him in a narrow lane ; he strove to pass her by, and did in much fear, as doubting what she might be. Some time after, having occasion to pass that way by night, he saw her in the same shape, and in the same dress ; he was afraid to pass by her ; but he was resolved to speak to her, and asked her what she wanted with him ? to which she bid him not to be afraid, that she would not hurt him. She told him he must go to *Philadelphia*, in *Pensylvania*, and take a box from a house there, which she described, (in which there was two hundred pounds) and charged him to meet her on the friday night following. He having declared this to some neighbours, the news reached the ears of the Curate of the Parish, who sent for this man to come to his house : they appointed a prayer-meeting to be that friday night, to which they desired the young man to come : the meeting continued till midnight, in which he was observed to be very uneasy to go out. When the meeting ended he went out with the Parson's servants to the horses, and in coming from the stable, he was taken from among them ; at which they were greatly amazed, not knowing what to think of it. But the Apparition carried him away to a river and threw him into it, chiding him for telling the people of the appointed meeting, and not coming to meet her according to promise ; but bid him not to be afraid, that she would not hurt him, because she had not charged him not to speak of her charge to meet her on friday night ; but that he should not have gone to the Parson's house.

Now, said she, we begin the journey : he was then lifted up and carried away he knew not how. When he came to the place, he was taken into a house, and then conducted to a fine room : the Spirit then bid him lift up a board, which he did ; he then saw the box, and took it, then the Spirit said he must go three miles and cast it into the black sea : they went, as he thought, to a lake of clear water, where he was commanded to throw the box into it ; which when he did there was such a noise as if all about was going to pieces : from thence he was taken up and carries to the place where he was first taken up. He the asked her whether he was free now ? She said he was, and told him a secret, which she strictly charged him to tell no person. He was three days and three nights in this mysterious journey ; that   was, from friday night to monday night : when he came home he could scarcely speak. As to *her* appearance, she was largely made, looked pale, her looks severe, and her voice hollow, different from a human voice. A woman in the neighbourhood remembered lately that one Elizabeth Gething went from this neigh-bourhood into *Pensylvania* : most likely it was her Spirit, which perhaps she told the young man.

A. D. after being in great trouble of mind for a long time, she at last hanged herself ; not long after, a young man, from *Lliwel* Parish, came to see a young woman (whom he courted) who lodged at the house of Thomas Richard, who was then from home ; he stayed there till very late that night, and then went to an ale-house, though he was per-suaded to stay : on going towards the ale-house, he saw a fire near a smith's shop the other side of the river ; presently he saw the fire in a field where he was to pass, which terrified him much, and he turned out of the way thinking to avoid it : but presently he saw a woman standing before him, whose shape and clothes he well remembered ; on seeing this, terrified him much, and he went to the ale-house faintly and indisposed. The woman of the house made him welcome, and put him to bed, suspecting he had seen an Apparition, and asked him about it ; which he owned he had. The next day he went home very ill ; and being out late at night, he saw her ; he came in and went to bed, and there he saw her by the bed side. A cousin of his (a young man) came to see him, and thinking his illness was nothing else but his being disappointed in his love affair, began to rally him about it ; merrily asked him has she refused thee ? To which his cousin soberly replying, and told him how it was. His cousin said thou must speak to her, or thou will not have quiet : I will go with thee and see thou shalt have no harm. They went out and called at *Tavarn y Carreg*, an inn so called ; but he could not drink, and often looked towards the door ; of which some who were in the house took notice, and asked what ailed the man ? But he was uneasy to go, so he went out, and his cousin followed him. As soon as he was out in the yard, he saw her ; it was the same woman who had hanged herself, and was now in the kingdom of darkness ; for no eternal life is promised to self-murderers, 1 *John* iii. 15. As soon as her saw her he said O God here she is ! upon which his cousin said this is a sad thing, I know not what to think of thee : but come, I will go with thee go where thou wilt. They both went into the ale-house where he had been at first, not far from the house where the unhappy woman had hanged herself. When he was in the house, and it was late at night, he began to be uneasy again, and said he must go out ; his cousin said he would go with him, and he said no, thou shalt not ; others also offered to go with him, but he said that no person should go with him. He went out, she appeared to him, but bid him not fear ; she said he must follow her. She led him to the back side of the house where she had lived, and bid him take from the wall a small bag, which he did ; it contained a great sum of money, supposed to be large pieces of gold ; he guessed might be about Two Hundred Pounds ; but he was in too much fear to look what they were : she bid him go and cast it into the river, which he did. Some persons, who heard of this, went to the river to see for the money, but they could find none.

The Rev. Mr. Thomas Lewis, who related to me this passage, saw the place where the money was hid, and wondered how the man could reach it, it being so very high ; but likely he was assisted by the Spirit. Mr. Lewis, then a dissenting minister in those parts, asked the young man what sort of voice she had, and whether it was not terrible ? He said it was of a dry sound, as if it were out of a drum, but not so terrible.

THE account of another very remarkable Apparition, in the Valley of *Tawey*, above *Ystrad-gynlas*, I had from Thomas Lewis, who knew the man who saw the Apparition, and was with him when he died. As he was employed by some Spirits to throw away hidden things in two or three places, there appeared to him, as he thought, a clergyman, dressed in black clothes, with a white wig on. Once when he was at an ale-house late in the evening, he saw him near the ale-house door, on horse back ; went out to him, and was seen pulling off his hat, bowing, offering drink, and saying to him, *Attoch chwi Syr*,---(towards you Sir) ; but the people could see nothing. Whether it was then or some other time, the Spectre strictly charged him to go to a Castle in *Radnorshire*, which he named, and take out of it some money that was concealed there, and throw it into the river, and threatened him severely if he did not do it, that he should have no rest. He was allowed to take a friend with him as far as the Castle, but only himself was to enter into it, and he was to make no stay with the money in his hand, but to run with it to the river. When they came near the Castle it was dark : but he was either lighted or guided by some Spirit to the place where the money was. He brought it out in haste, and ran with it, and cast it into the river.

ONE time a person was commanded by an Apparition, near a gentleman's house, in the County of *Glamorgan*, to take a box of money from some place in the house, and cast it into the river ; which he did. And in the same County there was another obliged to cast a trunk of copper money into the water, in order to have quiet from as Apparition.

In Cardiganshire.

The circumstance which I am going to relate is concerning SIR DAVID LLWYD, who lived near *Yspythi-Ystwyth*, in this County, who was a curate, likely of that Church, and a Physician ; but being known to deal in the Magic Art, he was turned out of the Curacy, and obliged to live by practising physic:

THERE was once a Tailor, a profane man, and a great drunkard, who having been to a Fair, and coming home drunk, met a certain man on horse back, who asked him if he were a Tailor ? He said he was : the man on horse back asked him if he would make some clothes for him ? He said he would, and received a piece of cloath with a charge to be sure to be at home on such a day, and such an hour, to take his measure : the Tailor said he would. Although he was drunk, he observed this person's feet were not like a man's, but like horse's feet ; and some other circumstances which made him concerned ; the more he considered it, his fear increased, thinking it was not a man, but something belonging to the devil ; he being in great fear about the matter, went to Sir David to ask his opinion about it, from whom he received the following advice :---to delay the measuring of him as much as possible, and not to stand before but behind him : he bid him be sure to be at home the time appointed, and that he (Sir David) would come to meet him that time. The supposed man came, and the Tailor, in great fear, began to

measure him, at the same time fearing he was something not good ; and according to the advice given
him, delayed measuring him, pretending that he
wanted this and that thing : at last the supposed man
said to him, thou art very long about it, and why
standest thou behind my back ? why dost thou not
come before me ? The Tailor being in greater fear,
thought every minute a long time, expecting Sir David
to come according to his promise ; accordingly he
came, and having looked on the strange man who was
come to be measured, said to him, What is your
business here ? Go away ; and he went away.
This the Tailor told to all who enquired about it, and
it passed through the Country.

Another time being gone on a visit towards the
Town of *Rhaiadr Gwy,* in *Radnorshire,* and being gone
from one house to another, but having forgotten his
Magic Book in the first house, sent his boy to fetch it,
charging him not to open the book on the way ; but
the boy being very curious opened the book, and the
evil Spirit immediately called for work ; the boy,
though surprised and in some perplexity, said, *Tafl
gerrig o'r Avon,*--- (throw stones out of the river), he
did so ; and after a while having thrown up many
stones out of the river Wye, or Elgy, which ran that
way, he again, after the manner of confined Spirits,
asking for something to do ; the boy had his senses
about him to bid it throw the stones back into the
river, and it did so. Sir David seeing the boy long in
coming, doubted how it was ; came back and chide
him for opening the book, and commanded the familiar
Spirit back into his book.

Another time being gone to *Lanidlos* Town, in
Montgomeryshire, twelve miles from home, and as he
was going home very late in the evening, seeing a boy
there of his neighbourhood, offered him to ride behind
him if he was for going home, which the boy accepted,
and they came home in about two hours. The boy
had lost one of his garters in the journey, but seeing
something hanging in the ash tree near the Church,

climbed up to see what it was, and to his great surprise he found it was his garter which he had lost ;
which shews they rode home in the air.

It was thought that he learnt the Magic Art privately
in *Oxford*, in the profane time of Charles the Second,
when many vices greatly prevailed. It was this man's
great wickedness to make use of a familiar Spirit, one
of the enemies of God and man ; a thing forbidden in
holy writ, *Lev*. xix. 31. Seeking counsel of a woman
who had a familiar Spirit, was one of the causes of
Saul's destruction, 1 *Chron*. x. 11.

The Bishop did well in turning him out of the
sacred office, though he was no ill-tempered man ; for
how unfit was such a man to read the sacred scripture,
especially those chapters where seeking after familiar
Spirits is forbidden and condemned ? How unfit to
read the good prayers of the Church, and to administer
the holy ordinances of God ? With what propriety
and conscience could he ask the Sponsers in baptism
to undertake for the child to renounce the world, the
flesh, and the devil, who himself was in covenant with
hell, and familiar with one of the Spirits of darkness ?
And how far from renouncing the devil and all his
works, as he had engaged to do ? And had told the
Bishop that he was moved by the Holy Ghost to seek
ordination to the holy office, to act against the kingdom of darkness.

Of this Sir David, I have heard several things ; but
chiefly depend upon what was related to me by the
Rev. Mr. Thomas Lewis, the Curate of *Landdw* and
Tolachdy, an excellent preacher of the gospel ; and
not sufficiently esteemed by his people, which likely
will bring a judgment upon them in time to come.

Mr. Lewis who gave me this relation, knew the
young woman who had been his maid servant, and
the house where she lived.

In   Pembrokeshire.

JOHN JENKIN, a school-master, and also a conjurer ; and being known to be such, one of his
scholars having a mind to it, told his master he had a
curiosity to see the devil ; his master told him he
might if he had courage for it ; but told him he did
not chuse to call an evil Spirit till he had some em-
ployment for him.   Some time after a man came to
him who had lost some money, and desiring to know
who had stolen it.   Now, said the master to the
scholar, I have some business for him.   That night the
conjurer and his scholar went into a wood and drew a
circle, then came home.   Some night after they went
into the circle, and the conjurer called an evil Spirit
by its name :   presently they perceived a light, and a
remarkable attitude in the sky : after that a ball of
light shot like lightening towards the circle, and turned
round about it ; the conjurer asked it who had stolen
such a man's money ? But by the answer which he
received he understood that *that* Spirit knew not who
had done it.   The master told the scholar that *that*
Spirit knew not who had done it, and that he must
call another : having sent that Spirit away he called
another ; and presently they saw the resemblance of a
Bull flying through the air towards them, and so
swiftly and fiercely as if it would go through them, and
it turned about the circle ; he asked it also who had
stolen the money ?   He received much the same kind
of answer as from the former.   The conjurer told his
scholar this also would not do,   I must call another.
After the young scholar was a little revived, (being
almost dead with fear) his master called another of
them by name ; and behold there came out of the
wood a Spirit dressed in white, and coming towards
the circle.   When the conjurer saw it, he told his
scholar we shall now hear something from this.   He
then asked it the same question ; the Spirit answered
he knew the person who had taken the said money ;
told him who he was, and other circumstances concerning that matter, which the conjurer asked it.   The

young man declared that neither those Spirits could speak to answer the conjurer until they had worked themselves into a human shape. The man has never been well since.---The effect of the great fright and of his presumption to see one of the fallen angels of hell under the curse and wrath of God still cleaving to him : so dangerous it is to have to do (especially in an extraordinary way) with those mortal enemies of mankind, divested of all remains of their created virtue an goodness. The servants of satan little consider this, else they would not chuse the life which goes after satan to endless misery, but the life that leads to Angels and the Spirits of just men made perfect, and to the God of all happiness.

NOT far from *Glanbran*, in *Carmarthenshire*, lived a Tailor, who was a conjurer ;--- he went to the house of one Mr. Gwynne, of *Glanbran*. Mr. Gwynne began to talk to him about his conjuring, rather in the way of blaming him. The conjurer being a little mean-looking man ; Mr. Gwynne said he wondered how such a man as he had the courage to look upon the devil ! Mr. Gwynne, either designedly, or inadvertedly, happened to ask, Canst thou show him to me ! To which the conjurer replied, You are not able to look at him. Mr. Gwynne said, What thou able to look at him, and not I ? The conjurer said, If you are able to look at him, I will shew him to you. The gentleman consenting, the conjurer went out (it was in the day time) and made a circle after the usual manner, in a little grove of wood in a field not far from the house : he called one of the fallen angels, now become a devil, into it ; and returned to fetch the gentleman to see him, who met him just at the door, and said to him, Come with me and you shall see him. He followed him to the stile which entered into the field where the horrible sight was, when the conjurer said to the gentleman, Look yonder, there it is ! As soon as the gentleman saw it, (there was something so horrible and terrible in the sight) he said to the man, Oh ! take him quickly out of my sight ; and so he did.

K

I do not remember having heard any thing amiss of this gentleman ; but if he did not believe the existence and Apparition of Spirits, he had a rare and doubtless effectual conviction to his infidelity.

LEWIS WILLIAM WALTER, a man of uncommon elevation of mind in the scientific way, and of great skill in medicine ; and John Matthew Howel, a person whom I know and spoke with ; his wife was a dissenter and a woman truly pious ; his daughters were also religious.   As they were drinking together in *Merthyr Tidfil* Village, in *Glamorganshire*, they both agreed to go to conjure ; the place they chose to go to,   was, by a wall side, which divided between the mountain and some fields, at some considerable distance from the Village.   Having drank very much, thinking it would put them in heart against the approaching terror, and being come to the place where they was to conjure ; Lewis being the greater proficient in the Black-Art, called one of the Infernal Spirits by name, ordering it to appear in the shape of a gosling ;   accordingly it came, and demanded why they sent for him ?   They having drank too much, their speech failed to give it a speedy answer ; it rose up like a flash of fire, which deprived Lewis William Walter of his eye-sight, whom John Mathew Howel was obliged to carry back, after loosing his most useful members : he went into the Village with great sorrow to himself and friends, and the amazement of all his neighbours.

Mr. D. W. of *Pembrokeshire*, a religious man,   and far from fear and superstition, gave me the following account :---that as he was travelling by himself through a field, called the *Cot-moor*,   where two stones are set up, called the *Devil's Nags*, at some distance from each other, where evil Spirits are said to haunt and trouble passengers, he was thrown over the hedge, and was never well afterwards.   Mr. W. went with a strong fighting Mastiff Dog with him ; but suddenly he saw another Mastiff Dog coming towards him.   He thought to set his Dog at it ; but his Dog seemed to be much frightened, and would not go near it. Mr. W. then stooped down to take up a stone, thinking to throw at it ; but suddenly there came a Fire round it so that he could perceive it had a white tail and a white snip down his nose, and saw his teeth grinning at him ; he then knew it was one of the Infernal Dogs of Hell.---One of those kind of dogs against whom David prayeth in *Psal.* xxii. 20. "Deliver my soul from the power of of the Dog".

AS Mr. D. W. was walking out one evening, he saw the likeness of a man, at some distance from him ; it had no hat on, neither could he perceive that it had any arms : it went round him three of four times ; but kept the same distance from him. Mr. W. spoke to it several times, asking it what it wanted, &c. but he received no answer. He thought it was some person that had lost the way, so he went out of the path thinking to give way to it ; but suddenly he was seized with such a terror, that he scarcely knew where he was : he proceeded on his journey till he came to a hill, some distance from the place of the Apparition ; and, on ascending up the hill, he looked back towards the place where the Apparition was,---there he saw a Ball of Fire. When he came to the house the people saw him look bad and discomposed ; they asked him if he had been frightened ? He was ready to faint, (though a strong man) therefore could give them no answer. They gave him some cordial which kept him from fainting, and recovered him from his trembling.

As the appearance of Angels is a sign of good, so I have observed the extraordinary Apparitions of evil Spirits, have often been signs of trouble to those that saw them ; as it came to pass upon this man, with a witness.

As an acquaintance of mine was going from *Lanhither* towards *Abergweidd*, in the Parish of *Mynythusloin*, one night, she saw a ball of fire as large as a pompion, skipping before her, out of which came forth flames about half-a-yard long. After some time it receded, and went by her side : sometimes it followed her, which terrified her much. Some part of the way it disappeared, then it appeared again ; continuing so several times, till it came into the Village, when it decreased to the size of a tennis ball, and then entered into a shop in the Village : ---this terrified the young woman so much, that when she came into the house she fainted.

In Carmarthenshire.

I am now come into that part of Wales where we shall meet with the most numerous, and most notable account of Apparitions.--- The middle part of the Bishoprick of *St. David's*, where the most important account of the *Corpse Candles*, and the *Kyhyrraeth*, are to be met with, than any other part of Wales, by far.

What I am now going to relate is concerning one of the most terrible Apparitions that I ever heard of, related to me by R. A. (a woman who appeared to me to be a true living experimental Christian, beyond many) in relation to herself, as follows :----

AS she was going to *Laugharn* Town, one evening, on some business, it being late, her mother dissuaded her from going, telling her it was late, and that she would be benighted ; likely she might be terrified by an Apparition, which was both seen and heard by many, and by her father among others, at a place called *Pant y Madog*, which was a pit by the side of the lane leading to *Laugharn*, filled with water, and not quite dry in the summer. However, she seemed not to be afraid, therefore went to *Laugharn* ; on coming back before night, (though it was rather dark) she passed by the place ; but not without thinking of the Apparition : but being a little beyond this pit, in a field where there was a little rill of water, and just going to pass it, having one foot stretched over it, and looking before her, she saw something like a great Dog (one of the Dogs of hell) coming towards her ; being within four or five yards of her, it stopped, sat down, and set up such a scream, so horrible, so loud, and so strong, that she thought the earth moved under her ; with which she fainted, and fell down ; she did not awake and go to the next house, which was but the length of one field from the place, until about midnight ; having one foot wet in the rill of water which she was going to pass when she saw the Apparition.   She was very weak that night ; and for a long time after a very loud noise would disturb, and sicken her.   She owned it was a just punishment for her presumption, and disobeying her good mother's advice.

WALTER WATKINS, of *Neuath*, in the Parish of *Landdetty*, in the County of *Brecon*, being at school at *Carmarthen*, and as he and some other scholars who lodged in the same house with him were playing ball by the house, late in the evening,   heard the dismal mournful noise of the *Kyhyrraeth*, very near them ; but could see nothing, which was very shocking to hear : though these sort of men are incredulous enough, yet they were soon persuaded that it was the voice of neither man nor beast, but of some Spirit, which made them leave their play and run into the house,   Not long after, a man who lived near the house died.   This kind of noise is always heard before some person's death.

The woman of the house where these scholars lodged, related to them many such accounts, which they heard with contempt and ridicule, believing nothing of what she said.   One morning they asked her, sportingly, what she had seen or heard of a Spirit that night ?   She readily answered, that she heard a Spirit come to the door, and passing by her while she sat by the fire ; it seemed to walk into a room where a sick man was, and after some time I heard it coming back, and as if it fell down in a faint, and was raised up again. Soon after the sick man rose up, thinking he was able to walk, came into the room where the woman heard the fall, and fell down dead in that very part of the room where the Spirit made the same kind of stir, which his fall made, and was made by those that raised him up. This made the scholars, who believed nothing of what she said before, believe every thing which she said afterwards ; for that which she related came to pass and that she could have no other way to fore-tell these things, but by some representations made to her from the world of Spirits. Thus these young men were cured of their evil inclination to sadduceism, and obliged by a kind of prophecy accomplished, and matter of fact, to believe the being of Spirits against their natural inclination to it. The said Walter Watkins told me, that he was sorry to hear the *Coed y Cymmar* and *Merthyr* dissenting proffessors, ridicule the account of Apparitions, and seeking to make so many honest men liars, who speak of Apparitions and the agencies of Spirits from the most sensible experience.

———

A Clergyman's son, in this County, but now a clergyman himself in England, who, in his younger days, was somewhat vicious ; having been at a debauch one night, and coming home late when the doors were locked, and the people in bed, feared to disturb them ; fearing also their chiding an expos-tulations about his staying so late, went to the servant who slept in an out room, as is often the manner in this Country ; he could not awake the servant, but while he stood over him, he saw a small light come out of the servant's nostrils, which soon became a *Corpse Candle* : he followed it out and it came to a foot bridge, which lay over a rivulet of water. It came into the gentleman's head to raise up the end of the foot bridge from off the bank whereon it lay, to see what it would do. When it came, it seemed to offer to go over, but did not go, as if loath to go because the bridge was displaced : when he saw that, he put the bridge in its place, and stayed to see what the *Candle* would do. It came on the bridge when it was replaced ; but when it came near him, it struck, as it were with an handkerchief ; but the effect was strong, for he became dead upon the place, not knowing of himself a long time before he revived : such is the power of the Spirits of the other world, and it is ill jesting with them. A sadducee and a proud ridiculer of Apparitions in this gentleman's place now, would have a pure seasoning for his pastime. 'Tis true these men have not seen the *Corpse Candles* of W ALES, but they should believe the numerous and ever continuing witnesses of it, and not foolishly discredit abundant matters of fact, attested by many honest wise men. We have heard of others, who, from an excess of natural courage, or being in liquor, have endeavoured to stop the Corpse Candles, and have been struck down upon the place : but now none offer it, being deterred by a few former examples related, remembered, and justly believed.

GEORGE GRIFFITH, of *Carmarthen*, enlisted in the Carmarthen Militia, and being gone to the West of England, at one time, while he was in bed , he received a terrible blow from an unseen agent ; soon after the Spirit of a tall man appeared to him, who told him he was a german, a mariner, and had stolen some iron, some money and some clothes, out of the ship he was in, and had hid them in the earth ; he persuaded George Griffith very much to go there and take them away ; telling him where they were, and promising he would trouble him no more ; for he often appeared to him whenever he could find him a secret place. At last, to have quiet from the extraordinary trouble, he was persuaded to go, it may be chiefly for the money, enlisted himself with some regulars, and went to the wars, in *Germany*. The Spirit told him he should not lose his life in the war, but should come back safe ; as indeed he came. He went to the place where the Spirit directed him, there he found the iron and twelve shillings, but the clothes were spoiled and good for nothing. The iron he sold, and the money he kept for his own use. When the Apparition parted from him, it bid him not fear ; but either shut his eyes and stand, or fall down with his face towards the earth. He chose the latter, and the Spirit parted from him with such a noise as if the world about him was going to pieces. He returned home, and is like one desirous to mend his life.

A WOMAN, in *Carmarthen* Town, protested to Mr. Charles Winter, of the Parish of *Bedwellty*, (who was then at the Academy, and since became a Preacher of the Gospel) that she heard like the sound of a company, as it were a burying coming up from a river, and presently as it were the sound of a cart coming another way to meet the company, and the cart seemed to stop while the company went by, and then went on : soon after a dead corpse was brought from the river from one of the vessels, and a cart met the burying, and stopped till the company passed by ; exactly as the woman heard. Mr. W. was no man to tell an untruth, and the woman no self-interest to serve by telling an untruth. The wonder is, how these Spirits can so particularly fore-show things to come ? Either their knowledge of future things near at hand, must be very great, or they must have a great influence to accomplish things as fore-shown. Be it either way, the thing is wonderful ! Of the very minute and particular knowledge of these Spirits in the manner of death and burials.

I am now going to give you an account of another remarkable instance, which is as follows :---

As a certain man was in a field burning turf, he saw the Fairies coming through the field where he lay blowing the fire in one of the pits ; they went by him like a burial, imitating the singing of psalms as they went ; one of them leaped over his legs. He rose up to see where they would go, and followed them into a field which led into a wood : soon after a real burying came through that field, and he lay down by the pit of turf to see what they would do, and one of the company actually leaped over his legs in passing by, just as one of the Fairies had done before ; and they sung psalms at the burial as the Fairies fore-shewed.

AS two women, methodists, from *Ystrad gynlas* Parish, was going towards *Ty Gwyn*, in the Parish of *Llangadog*, Carmarthenshire, where there lived one John Williams ; they heard the voice of one singing psalms coming to meet them ; they new the voice to be the voice of John Williams ; when the voice came near them, it slackened and grew weak ; when it came within about twenty yards distance, just over against them, the passing voice ceased, yet was soon renewed ; and when about twenty yards distant, the singing was as strong as before : they heard some of the words which was from *Psal.* 105 : they did not hear all the words, but the beginning and end of the stanzas. The next Lords day, at the dissenting meeting, at *Coome Llyfynallt*, to their great astonishment, they heard that very psalm given out by John Williams, and sung. When

L

they heard this, they said one to another, that is the voice and the words we heard sung on the way. The fifth Lord's day after John Williams was buried.---This was another notable instance both of the being and fore-knowledge of Spirits.

JOSHUA COSLET, a man of sense and knowledge, told me of several *Corpse Candles* he had seen, but of one in particular which he saw in a lane, called *Heol bwlch y gwynt*,---(Wind gap lane)---in *Landeilo Fawr* Parish ; where he suddenly met a *Corpse Candle*, of a small light when near him, but increasing as it went farther from him.   He could easily perceive that there was some dark shadow passing along with the *Candle* ; but he was afraid to look earnestly upon it.   Not long after a burying passed that way.   He told me that it is the common opinion, doubtless from some experience of it, that if a man should wantonly strike it, he should be struck down by it ; but if one touches it unawares, he shall pass on unhurt.   He also said that some dark shadow of a man carried the *Candle*, holding it between his three fore fingers over against his face.   This is what some have seen, who had the courage to look earnestly.   Others have seen the likeness of a *Candle* carried in a skull.   There is nothing unreasonable or unlikely in either of these representations.

ONE William John, of the Parish of *Lanboydi*, a smith, on going home one night, being somewhat drunk and bold, (it seems too bold) saw one of the *Corpse Candles* ; he went out of his way to meet with it, and when he came near it, he saw it was a burying, and the corpse upon the bier, the perfect resemblance of a woman in the neighbourhood whom he knew, holding the *Candle* between her fore fingers, who dreadfully grinned at him ; and presently he was struck down from his horse, where he remained a while, and was ill a long time after before he recovered. This was before the real burying of the woman. His fault, and therefore his danger, was his coming presumptuously against the *Candle.*---This is another sensible proof of the Apparition and being of Spirits.

R. D. a good wise religious woman, gave me this remarkable account of one Reylold,---a young man, who hearing it affirmed, as usually it is in that Country, that, if any person watched in any church porch for a night, they would see those that would be buried that year come in at the church to be buried. One that did so, at last saw himself come in, as was said, and he died that year. Having drank much to put himself in heart, he ventured to go to the porch of the meeting-house at *Henllan-Amgoed*, (there being a burying yard by that meeting-house) and having sat there some time, there came a thick mist that darkened the place, and filled him with terror : he left the place, and when he came home, behold his hair on that side of his head which was next to the Apparition, tho' he saw only a dark mist, was turned white, and remained so all his days. She who related the story to me, saw him, and I asked what sort of hair he had , and she said it was a lank hair, and turning a little at the end. She thinks he was a sober minded man, if not truly religious ; and seemed penitent for his presumption. What he did indeed was no perfect necromancy, for he did not seek any thing of the dead as Saul did, but it was a thing that bordered on it. This could not but be known in all the Country round about ; and it is a strong confutation of Sadduceism ; for here is the testimony of a sober man, and the change of his hair against this unreasonable kind of incredulity, tho' it is but one of a thousand that might easily be found against it.

Let none think ill of *Henllan* meeting upon this
account ; for there is no place so sacred below
heaven but Satan can come near it, and into it ; for
he came into paradise, a more sacred place & a type
of heaven.   The *Henllan* congregation is one of the
largest in Wales, much about four hundred commu-
nicants, and contains abundance of good people :
having had also excellent ministers to serve them.
Messrs.   Henry Palmer, Thomas Morgan, John
Powell,   and Mr. Richard Morgan,   one of the best
ministers   now   in   WALES.

T H E   for knowledge   of those *Corpse Candle*
Spirits, concerning deaths and burials, is wonderful,
particular as the following instance will shew :---

One Rees Thomas, a carpenter, passing through
a place called *Rhiw Edwst,* near *Cappel Ewen,* by
night, heard a stir coming towards him, walking
and speaking ; and when they were come to him he
felt   as   if some person put their hand upon his
shoulder, and saying to him, *Rhys bach pa fodd yt
y'ch chwi* ?---(Dear Rees, how are you) ?   which
surprised him much ; for he saw nothing.   But a
month after, passing that way, he met a burying in
that very place ; and a woman who was in the company, put her hand upon him and spoke exactly the
same words to him that the invisible Spirit had spoken to him before ; at which he could no less than
wonder.   This I had from the mouth of, Mr. T. I.
of *Trevach* a godly minister of the gospel.

The   following account I had from under the
hand of Mr. Morris Griffith, a man truly religious,
and a lively preacher of the gospel, among the
Baptists ; which came to pass in Pembrokeshire,
as follows :---

When I kept School at *Pont-Faen* Parish, in
Pembrokeshire, as I was coming from a place called

Tre-Davith, and was come to the top of the hill, I saw a great light down in the Valley, which I wondered at ; for I could not imagine what it meant. But it came to my mind that it was a light before a burying, though I never could believe before that there was such a thing. The light which I saw then was a very red light, and it stood still for about a quarter of an hour in the way which went towards *Lanferch-llawddog* church. I made haste to the other side of the hill, that I might see it farther ; and from thence I saw it go along to the church yard, where it stood still for a little time, and entered into the church : I stood still waiting to see it come out, and it was not long before it came out, and went to a certain part of the church-yard, where it stood a little time, and then vanished out of my sight.

A few days afterwards, being in school with the children about noon, I heard a great noise over head, as if the top of the house was coming down ; I went out to see the garret, and there was nothing amiss. A few days afterwards, Mr. Higgon, of *Pont-Faen*'s son died. When the carpenter came to fetch the boards to make the coffin, which were in the garret, he made exactly such a stir in handling the boards in the garret, as was made before by some Spirit, who fore-knew the death that was soon to come to pass. In carrying the body to the grave, the burying stood where the light stood for about a quarter of an hour, because there was some water cross the way, and the people could not go over it without wetting their feet, therefore they were obliged to wait till those that had boots helped them over. The child was buried in that very spot of ground in the church-yard, where I saw the light stop after it came out of the church. This is what I can boldly testify, having seen and heard what I relate :---a thing, which before, I could not believe,

Morris Griffith.

Before the light of the Gospel prevailed, there were in *Carmarthenshire* and elsewhere often heard before burials what by some were called *Cwn Annwn*,---(Dogs of Hell) : by others *Cwn bendith eu Mammau*,---(Dogs of the Fairies) : and by some *Cwn wybir*,---(Sky Dogs). The nearer they were to a man, the less their voice was,---like that of small beagles ; and the farther the louder : and sometimes like the voice of a great hound sounding among them, like that of a blood-hound,--- a deep hollow voice.

ONE Thomas Phillips, of *Trelech* Parish, heard those Spiritual Dogs, and the great Dog sounding among them ; and they went in a way which no corpse used to go ; at which he wondered, as he knew they used to go only in the way in which the corpse was to go. Not long after a woman who came from another Parish, that died at *Trelech*, was carried that way to her own Parish church to be buried, in the way in which those Spiritual Dogs seemed to hunt.

AN acquaintance of mine, a man perfectly firm to tell the truth, being out at night heard a hunting in the air, and as if they overtook something which they hunted after, and being overtaken made a miserable cry among them, and seemed to escape ; but overtaken again, made the same dismal cry ; and again escaped, and followed after till out of hearing.

Some have been so hardy as to lye down by the way side where the Corpse-Candle passed, that they may see what passed ; for they were not hurted who did not stand in the way. Some have seen the resemblance of a skull carrying the Candle, others the shape of the person that is to die carrying the Candle between its fore-fingers, holding the light before its face, Some have said that they saw the shape of those who were to be at the burying. I am willing to suspend my belief of this as seeming to be extravagant, though their fore-boding knowledge of mortality appears to be very wonderful and undeniable.

I am now going to give you an account of the *Kyhirraeth*, a doleful fore-boding noise before death, and enquire into the cause of this, and of the appearance of the Corpse-Candles.

D. P. Of *Lan y Byther* Parish, a sober sensible man and careful to tell the truth, informed me that in the beginning of the night, his wife and maid-servant being together in the house, which was by the way side, they heard the doleful voice of the *Kyhirraeth :* and when it came over against the window, it pronounced these strange words of no signification, that we know of,---*Woolach, Woolach :* and sometime after a burying passed that way. I confess a word of this sound, especially the latter part of the last syllable sounding in Welsh like the twentythird letter of the Greek Alphabet, at least as they pronounced it formerly in the schools, pronounced by a Spirit of the night near at hand, with a disagreeable horrid sounding voice, was very terrible and impressive upon the mind and memory. The judicious Joshua Coslet, who lived on that side of the river *Towy* which runs through the middle of *Carmarthenshire*, where the *Kyhirraeth* is often heard, gave me the following remarkable account of it :---

That it is a doleful disagreeable sound heard before the deaths of many, and most apt to be heard before foul weather : the voice resembles the groaning of sick persons who are to die ; heard at first at a distance, then comes nearer, and the last near at hand ; so that it is a three-fold warning of death, ---the king of terrors. It begins strong and louder than a sick man can make, the second cry is lower, but not less doleful, but rather more so ; the third yet lower and soft, like the groaning of a sick man, almost spent and dying ; so that a person well remembering the voice, and coming to the sick man's bed who is to die, shall hear his groans exactly alike, which is an amazing evidence of the Spirits' fore-knowledge. Sometimes when it cries very loud, it bears a resemblance of one crying who is troubled with a stitch. If it meets any hindrance in the way, it seems to groan louder. It is, or hath been very common in the three Commots of *Ynis-Cenin*. A Commot is a portion of ground less than a Canttref, or a Hundred ; for three Commots make up the Hundred of *Ynis-Cenin*, which extends from the sea as far as *Landilo-Fawr* ; containing twelve Parishes, viz,--- *Landilo-Fawr, Bettws, Lanedi, Lannon, Cydweli, Langenich, Pen-fre, Lanarthney, Langyndeirn,* &c. which lie on the south-east side of the river *Towy*, where sometime past it cried and groaned before the death of every person, as my informant thought, who lived that side of the County. It sounded before the death of persons who were born in these Parishes and died elsewhere. Sometimes the voice is heard long before death, yet three quarters of a year is the longest time before hand ; but it must be a common thing indeed, as it came to be a common thing for people to say, by way of reproach, to a person making a disagreeable noise, *Oh 'r Kyhirraeth :* and sometimes to children crying and groaning unreasonable.

In the *Corpse Candles* and the *Kyhirraeth,* therefore we have a double testimony of the being of Spirits, and the immortality of the soul. The one to the eyes, and the other to the ears of men : continued through a long course of time, giving no place to the opposite infidelity.

But let us enquire into the cause of this. The prevailing opinion is, that it is an effect of St. David's prayer ; some will say of some other Bishop ; but the more intelligent think it of St. David, and none indeed so likely as St. David. St. D. was the most famous Saint in WALES, who did great things in his time ; for he put down the Pelagian heresy, in a Synod at *Caredigion,* now *Cardiganshire* ; and it was owing to his presence, prayers, and direction, that K. Arthur, and the Brittains overthrew the Saxons in a great Battle, at Bath, &c.

Being a very spiritual man, and living much under a sense of eternity, after his short life, as all very spiritual men do, and observing that the people in general were careless of the life to come, and could not be thought to mind it, and make a preparation for it, though he laboured much to bring them to it, prayed to God to give a sign of the immortality of the soul, and of a life to come, a presage of death, and a motive to prepare for it; and God, in answer to his prayer, sent the *Corpse Candles*, and likely the *Kyhirraeth* to answer the same pious end. This is the tradition in the Country about it ; and this is the only likely thing, for no other reason can be given for it, and it hath answered this good end ; for in those parts the opposite infidelity prevails not, at least among the common people ; and if it doth with some others who are hardened and abandoned. it will greatly aggravate their sin. Let no one think it in-credible that any man's prayers should be answered for so long a time, seeing the Lord promised to Jonadab the son of Rechab, a holy man in an evil time, that there should not fail one of his seed to stand before him for ever, *Jer.* xxxv. St. David had one of the best of ends in making this kind of prayer ; and if he had not, God would not have answered his prayer, and for so long a time. Some say that this came to pass in answer to the prayers of some Bishop, but that Bishop could be no other but St. David ; because it is in his Bishoprick they chiefly appear, and but seldom out of it. As for the *Kyhirraeth* being chiefly heard in the Commots or Hundreds of *Ynis-Cenin* ; the reason may be because Non the mother of St. David, a holy woman of God, like Nonica the mother of St. Austin, lived in those parts, called by her name *Lan-non*,---(Non's Church) and that also we are told in old writings, that she heard Gildas preaching at *Lan-morfa.*

In those parts when she was with child of St.David, she also might join with her son in his prayers, and desire as yet a farther sign for the same good end ; this is the most likely account of the matter.

And now what great evidence of the being of Spirits, the immortality of the soul, and of a world to come, have we in the appearance of the *Corpse Candles*, and the voice of the *Kyhirraeth*, since the days of St. David,

M

in the space of above a thousand years, and therefore seen and heard by many thousands of people.
If the *Corpse Candles* are less seen now, and the
Kyhirraeth not so often heard, it is very easy to
give a reason for it; for now the gospel which
brings life and immortality to light, 1 *Tim*. i. 10.
having greatly prevailed in WALES, and more especially in the Bishoprick of St. David, makes these
things far less necessary than before, and is the
reason of their being less frequent.

These *Corpse Candles* are sometimes seen elsewhere, for I saw one in the Town of *Wrexham*, in
Denbighshire, before the death of a lad in the
adjoining house where I lodged.

In Glamorganshire.

The following is an account of the wonderful actings of a disembodied
Spirit, which came to pass in the house of MR. WM. THOMAS.
in *Tridoll* Valley, not far from the Town of *Aberavan*.---The
account I had in a letter from the Rev. MR. WM. EVANS, of
Lanquake, who was there, & had it from them verbatim, as follows :

MR. Thomas's maid-servant durst no go with
the candle about the room by night, for the
light of the candle would diminish, grow narrow as
if in a damp, and at last would go out, and the fire
out of the wick, so that she was obliged to go to
the room without a light. When she came down
stairs, something would strike her on the side of her
head, as it were with a cushion. While she was at
private prayers, it would let her alone, excepting
once or twice that she was obliged to give over,
though a very courageous young woman. One
time she brought a marment of water into the house,
and the water rose up out of the vessel about her,
and about the house. Another time when abundance of pilchards came to the sea, so that the

people could scarce devour them, the mistress and
maid desirous to have some of them, she asked
leave of her master to go and fetch some of them;
but he being a very just man, told her not to go,
that the pilchards were sent for the use of poor
people, and that they themselves wanted nothing;
but she ventured to go, and brought some to the
house; but after giving a turn about the house, and
going to look after them, found them all gone, and
thrown upon the dunghill; upon which her master
blamed her, saying, Did not I tell thee not to go?
One time they had a pot of meat upon the fire, and
both the meat and broth were taken away, they
knew not where, and the pot left empty, to their no
small disappointment. Sometimes the clasped Bible
would be thrown wisking by their heads, and strik-
ing against something, and yet the Bible not much
damaged. So it would do with the gads of the
steller; and once it struck one of them against the
screen where a person then sat, and the mark of it
still to be seen in the hard board; such a blow in
the forehead, or temples, would have killed him on
the spot; but it did not touch the man which sat in
the screen. Once the china dishes were thrown off
the shelf, and not one broke. In divers particulars
the evil Spirit was evidently limited in its mischievous doings.

It troubled the maid very much in winter, taking
away the clothes from her bed; in summer, gather-
ing more clothes to put upon her bed. Sometimes
when it began to take off the clothes, she would
take hold and get upon them, and go to prayer;
and when she prayed, it would let the clothes alone
for that time; which encouraged her the more to
prayer. It was a great business with this light-hating
Spirit to throw an old lanthorn about the house
without breaking it. It would throw the candlestick
also, and yet the candle would not go out of the
socket, nor break.

M 2

Once she was going upon business before day, and being come into the highway, a thick darkness, which was terrible to enter into, filled the way ; upon which she thought once to go over the hedge to avoid it ; but presently thought it was not good to yield to the evil Spirit, and therefore went to prayer by the hedge-side ; after she rose up, the darkness went off, and she went her way. One night it divided the books among them, when they were in bed ; to the man of the house it brought the Bible, to the woman of the house Allen's Sure Guide, Arthur Dent, and such books as she delighted in ; upon the maid's bed the English books which she understood not. When it began to stir in the beginning of the night, the man of the house would call the family to prayer.

For about two years it troubled the whole of the family ; in which space of time, it would sometimes be quiet for a fortnight, or three weeks, giving no trouble. Once it endeavoured to hinder them from going to meeting, by hiding the bunch of keys, ad carrying them out of their place, on the Lord's day ; and for all their searching, could not find them. They were loath to appear in their old clothes at meeting. The good man of the house bid them not yield to the devil, but to borrow some clothes of one another ; something which one had, which another had not ; but at last there was something wanted which they could not be without, and must have or break the lock ; but concluded to go first to prayer, and so did, and afterwards found the keys where they used to be, and where they had searched enough for them before. Another time the maid went to milking to the barn, and while she was milking the cow, the barn-door was suddenly shut ; she rose up to see what had shut it, but could see nothing, and came back to milk ; then it turned the door backwards and forwards to make an

idle ringing noise ; she then knew what it was, and
before she had done milking shut the door ; but
when she attempted to open it afterwards, she could
not open it by any means ; and was going to open
another door, but presently thought it might hold
that fast shut ; therefore she went to prayer, thinking it was the best way of prevailing over the evil
Spirit ; and afterwards the door opened as usual.

One time it endeavoured to make variance between the mistress and the maid, by strewing char-
coal-ashes upon the milk ; when the mistress found
the milk so, she charged the maid with some neglect,
and watched the next milk herself ; yet this was
made more foul. At one time W. Thomas and his
wife went to watch to a neighbour's house, where
a relation of theirs lay dead. There was a young
man, a first cousin to William Thomas, who would
by no means believe that there was a Spirit at
W. T's house, and said they were only making
tricks with one another ; and very strong he was, a
hero of an unbeliever, like many of his brethren in
infidelity ; and said he would lie in the house alone,
and desired the keys of the house ; he had them, and
went to see if there was any Spirit in it ; but he had
no disturbance, and if he was strong before, so
strong that the testimony of three sober religious
persons had no weight with him ; he was now strong
with a witness, and very conceited in his own opinion, and bantered them upon it. Sometime after
he came and stayed over night ; and hearing that the
maid was disturbed in bed by the Spirit, he said,
in the hearing of the family, if any thing comes to
disturb thee, call upon me, he lying either in that
or the next room. Sometime in the night the Spirit
came to attempt to take away the clothes from the
maid, and she cried out ; he awaked and suddenly
rose out of bed, thinking to catch somebody who
was playing tricks with the maid, as he thought ; but

saw now that there was nothing to be with her ; but was made to know that there was an invisible agent in the place, which now severely handled him ; for feeling is believing. He went to his bed in a worse condition than he came out of it, excepting that he was cured of his stubborn sadducism. He never afterwards bantered them, being made to believe that there was something more than human in the place.

One time Mr. W. E. the author of this letter, being there, and at prayer by the bed side, it struck the bed so violently, though it was but with a trencher, that it made a report like that of a gun, so that both the bed and the room did shake ; it did so twice, which greatly surprised him. One time it made so great a noise, that the man of the house, on a sudden, thought the house was going away, and he was greatly terrified. It never after this made so loud a noise. Once, when they were at meeting, it threw the pad against the door at the foot of the stairs, which made so great a noise, as surprised and terrified them all, especially those who were near the door.

One time the Rev. Mr. R. Tibbet, a dissenting minister, from Montgomeryshire, coming to preach that way, he was an evangelical holy minister of Christ, came into this house, and being in bed together with another person, and expecting the stir, continued awake and talking a long time ; at last Mr. Tibbot slept ; his companion keeping awake heard it come, and awaked Mr. Tibbot. It began to pluck the clothes ; they held them, and prayed, and it let them alone a while. They being thoroughly awaked by this time, kept awake, expecting it would come again to pull the clothes, and turned the clothes about them as well as they could ; accordingly it came to pull them, which they held with all their might, so that they thought the clothes were broken between them ; which really they were not. Having not prevailed this way, it struck the bed with the cawnnen,---a vessel to hold corn, so strongly that it removed the bed out of its place, and with so loud a stroke that W. T. heard

it, and brought light with him ; they had quiet the
rest of the night. They had been keeping the day
before in a day of fasting and praying, which, it
may be, enraged it.

It deserves to be observed how this evil Spirit was
limited in its ill doings ; for when the good man of the
house, and such he certainly was, was shaving, it
would not touch him while the razor was on his face ;
but when he would take it off, it would strike him on
the side of his head.

The manner of its going away, and ceasing to
trouble, was this.---The man of the house being in bed
with his wife, thought he heard a voice calling him,
he then awaked her, and rose up a little in bed, and
said to the Spirit, in the name of the Lord Jesus what
seekest thou in my house ? Hast thou any thing to
say to me ? The Spirit answered, it had, and desired
him to remove some things, telling what they were,
out of the place where they had been mislaid. The
good man thinking it to be a devil, one of the fallen
angels, made answer, satan, I'll do nothing that thou
biddest me any farther than my bible gives me leave ;
I command thee, in the name of God, to depart from
my house. Both of them perfectly knew the voice to
be that of a relation of theirs who was dead, at least
that it perfectly resembled it. This gave them both a
great concern, least it should be the Spirit of that
relation of whom they hoped better things ; however,
from that time forth, it gave no disturbance. For my
part, I believe it was the disembodied Spirit of that
relation which sought an aleviating circumstance to its
bad state by the removal of those mislaid things, and
wish they had removed them ; as it always gives ease
to them who appear on such occasions, and cease to
give trouble to those to whom they appear ; there
being no reason to be given why one of the fallen
angels, properly called devils, should personate a
disembodied human Spirit, but reason against it. It
was the voice of a female relation, more nearly related
to Mr. than Mrs. Thomas, which they heard. Oh

that both men and women were more concerned, and laboured to the utmost to avoid a miserable, and to secure a happy eternity, after life and death.

The Conclusion Inferred from these Accounts.

A R E not all these numerous instances together sufficient to convince all the sadducees and atheistical men of the age, of the being of Spirits, and of their appearance in the world ? Surely one would think they are.

Will nothing serve the prevailing human corruption, but either the over believing things that have no reality ? Believing things more than they are ; or the not believing things that really are ; or as far as they are, and have a being against the necessity of believing them in order to felicity ? Some are so reduced in the the faculty and exercise of believing, that they scarce believe their own existence, and some deny their own Spirits, and say they are mere machines ; so strong hath unbelief prevailed in the world, that the faculty of believing, which God created in the understanding of the first man, the parent of mankind, is so impaired in many of his fallen posterity, as to be in some nearly anihiliated into nothing ! and in all mankind by nature so weak, that it cannot believe the things necessary to salvation without being repaired by the special grace of God ; for which cause faith is called the gift of God to salvation, *Eph.* ii. 5, 8, &c. The instances produced in this book, prove sufficiently the being of Spirits, of angels, and men, good and bad ; this again helps to believe the being of God, who is a Spirit, and the Father of the Spirits of all flesh, *Num.* xxvii. 15, 16. and should influence the lives of men in order to a due preparation for the future world, & immortality.

Apparitions

OF GOOD

S P I R I T S.

I AM now going to give an account of another kind of Apparitions, which came to pass in a time of persecution upon the dissenters in King Charles the Second's time.

There lived at a place called the *Pante*, which is between *Carmarthen* and *Laugharn* Towns, one Mr. David Thomas, a holy man, who worshiped the Lord with great devotion and humility ; he was also a gifted brother, and sometimes preached. On a certain night, for the sake of privacy, he went into a room which was out of the house, but nearly adjoining to it, in order to read and pray ; and as he was at prayer, and very highly taken up into a heavenly frame, the room was suddenly enlightened, and to that degree that the light of the candle was swallowed up by a greater light, and became invisible ; and with, or in that light, a company of Spirits, like children, in bright clothing, appeared very beautiful and sung ; but he recollected only a few words of it,--- (*Pa hyd ? Pa hyd ?   Dychwelwch feibion Adda,---* (How long ?   How long ?   Return ye sons of Adam) ; something like *Psal.* xc. 3.   After a time

N

he lost sight of them ; the light of the candle again came to appear, when the great light of the glorious company was gone. He was immersed in the heavenly disposition, and he fell down to thank and praise the Lord ; and while he was at this heavenly exercise, the room enlightened again ; the light of the candle became invisible, and the glorious company sung ; but he was so amazed at what he saw and heard, that he could remember only the following words, *Pa hyd ? Pa hyd yr crlidiwch y crist'nogion duwiol ?*---(How long ? How long will ye persecute the godly christians) ?   After a while they departed, and the candle-light appeared.   Any christian who enjoyed much of God's presence, will easily believe that David Thomas was now lifted up very high in the spiritual life, by this extraordinary visitation from heaven.

Here appears no gingle in the singing, so that it appears like the anthem-way of singing, or rather after the manner of the ancient Hebrews, in which there was little or no gingle, but tunes adjusted to the parts, and measure of the words sung.   After this he appeared to be greatly mortified to the things of time.   He did not speak much ; yet seemed to be a full vessel.   He seemed to care little but for the things of the spiritual world, and like one who had a constant calmness and serenity in his mind.   Christians who have had the extraordinary presence of God in a less measure than Mr. Thomas, do know from their own experience that it leaves a serious humble sweet calmness after it, which continues to part of the next day.

The sons of infidelity will question the truth, and cannot believe that the angels of heaven did thus appear to any man, & some of the boldest and crudest of them may mock and ridicule the account.

Did not the angels of God appear to many in times of old, to Abraham, Lot, Jacob, Gideon, Manoah, David, Zechariah, Cornelius, &c. ? I grant there is less necessity, and therefore they more seldom appear now when revelation is complete.   Doth not the apos-

tle say to the christians of the the New Testament, "Ye
" are come to Mount Zion, To the Spirits of just
" men made perfect, and to thousands of angels, &c."?
Heb. xii. 22, 23.   i. e. Ye are come through the
grace of the gospel dispensation into union and communion with the members and company of the church
above.   Is it unreasonable to think that some of them
may, upon some occasions, appear to some of their
friends below ?   They are said to serve the heirs of
salvation, *Heb*. i. 14.   And to protect the saints,
Psal. xxxvi. 7.   And is it unreasonable to think that
they should sometimes appear,   upon great occasions,
to their friends whom they serve ?   There are reasons
for their appearing sometimes to evidence the kind-
ness of God administered through them, and to help
the belief of it

I am now going to relate a circumstance which I
heard several times, from the mouths of several religious persons,   concerning Rees David,   a man of
more than common piety, who lived in the County
of *Carmarthen*, towards the lower end of it, inclining
towards Pembrokeshire ;   that at the time of his death,
and a little before his death, several persons who
were in the room heard, just as the time of his disso-
lution approached,   the singing of angels drawing
nearer and nearer ;   and after his death they heard the
pleasant incomparable singing gradually depart until
it was was out of hearing.   Here was no deception, for
several religious people, men of certain probity and
sincerity, heard and attested it, and the news of it
spread far, and was by no means discredited by those
who knew and heard of this holy man.   I also heard
it from some of the ministers of the gospel.

I think it not improper to relate a circumstance
which came to pass in the day of his burial, which
I chuse to apprehend as a sign of his happiness, and
so it was understood by those who saw it, and by
him,--a truly good man, and a preacher of the gospel,
who related it to me ; he was there present and saw it.

It was this,---before the body was brought forth, a white dove came and alighted upon the bier, in the presence and among all the company.

THE following is a notable account of a certain person's conversation with evil Spirits to his own ruin, in a letter sent to the Bishop of *Gloucester*, by the Rev. Mr. Arthur Bedford, Minister of Temple Parish, in *Bristol* :---

"BRISTOL, August 2, -------."

" My Lord,"

       " Being informed by Mr. Shutes of your Lordship's desire, that I should communicate to you what I had known concerning a person who was accquainted with Spirits to his own destruction ; I have made bold to give you the trouble of this letter, hoping my design to gratify your Lordship in every particular, may be an apology for the length hereof. I had formerly given an account to the late Bishop of *Hereford*, in which there may be some things contained which I do not now re-member ; which, if your Lordship could pro-cure from his Lady, who lives near *Gloucester*, would be more authentic."

" Whilst I was Curate to Dr. Read, Rector of St. Nicholas, in this City, I began to be acquainted with one Thomas Parkes, a young man about 20 years of age, who lived with his father at *Mangots-field*, in Gloucestershire, and by trade a Gunsmith, with whom I contracted an intimate acquaintance ; he being not only a good tempered man, but extremely well skill'd in the Mathematical studies, which was his constant delight, viz. Arithmetic, Geometry, Guaging, Surveying, Astronomy, and Algebra. He gave himself up to to Astronomy so far that he could not only calculate the motions of the Planets, but an Eclipse also, and demonstrate also every problem in Spherical Trigonometry from Mathematical principles, in which he would discover a clear force of reason. When Mr. Baily, Minister of St. James, in the City, endeavoured to set up a Mathematical Academy, I advised him to this Thomas Parkes, as an acquaintance ; in whom, as he told me, he found greater proficiency in those studies than he expected, or could have imagined. After this he applyed himself to Astrology, and would sometimes calculate Nativities, and resolved Horary questions, which he told me often times proved true ; but he was not satisfied with it, because there was nothing in it which tended to Mathematical demonstration. When by the providence of God I was settled in Temple Parish, and having not seen him for some time, he came to me, and we being in private, he asked my opinion very seriously concerning the lawfulness of conversing with Spirits. After I had given my thoughts in the negative, and confirmed them with

the best reasons I could, he told me he had considered all those arguments, and believed they only
related to conjuratism ; but that there was an innocent society with them which a man might use, if
he made no compact with them, did no harm by
their means, and was not curious in prying into
hidden things ; and that he himself had discoursed
with them, and heard them sing to his great satis-
faction.   He gave an offer to me at one time, to
Mr. Baily at another, that if we would go with him
one night to *Kingswood*, we should see them, hear
them talk and sing, and talk with them whatsoever
we had in mind to, and we should return very safe ;
but neither of us had the courage to venture.   I told
him of the subtilty of the devil to deceive mankind,
and to transform himself into an angel of light ; but
he could not believe it was the devil.   I proposed
to try him a question in Astronomy relating to the
projection of the Sphere, which he projected and
resolved ;   and afterwards did so demonstrate them
from the Mathematics as to demonstrate that his
brain was free from the least tincture of madness
and distraction.   I asked him several particulars
concerning the method he used, and the discourse
he had with the Spirits he conversed with.   He told
me he had a book where there was the directions
he followed ;   accordingly in the dead time of the
night he went into a cause-way with candle and
lanthorn, which was consecrated for the purpose
with incantations.   He had also consecrated chalk

consisting of several mixtures, with which he used
to   make a circle of what distance he thought fit,
within which circle no Spirit had power to enter.
After he invoked the Spirit by several forms of words,
some of which he told me were taken from the
holy scripture, and therefore he thought them lawful ; without considering that they might, as the
apostle saith, " *Pet.* iii. 16.   " be wrested to his
own destruction."   Accordingly the Spirits for
which he called, appeared to him in the shape of
little girls, about a foot and a half high, and played
about the circle.   At first he was affrighted, but
after some small acquaintance this antipathy in
nature wore off, and he became pleased with their
company.   He told me they spake with a shrill
voice,   like an ancient woman."

" He asked them if there was a God ; they told
him there was.   He asked if there was an heaven
and hell ; they said there was.   He asked what sort
of a place heaven was ; which they described as a
place of glory and happiness.   He asked what place
hell was ; and they bade him ask no questions of
that nature, for it was a dreadful thing to relate.
"The devils believe and tremble."   He asked what
method or order they had among themselves ; they
told him they were divided into three orders ; that
their chief had his residence in the air----that he had
several counsellors which were placed by him in
form of a globe, and he in the centre, which is the
chiefest order. Another order, they said, is em-

ployed in going to and fro from thence to the earth
to carry intelligence from those lower Spirits.
And a third order was in the earth according to the
directions they receive from those in the air.   This
description was very surprising ; but being contrary
to the account we have in scripture hierarchy of the
blessed angels, made me conclude they were devils ;
but I could not convince him thereof.   He told me
he had desired them to sing, and they went to some
distance behind a bush, from whence he heard a
perfect consort of such music, the like he never
heard ; and in the upper part he could hear something very harsh and shrill like a reed, but as it was
managed it came with particular grace."

"About a quarter of a year after he came to me
again, and said, he wish he had taken my advice ;
for he thought he had done that which would cost
him his life, and which he did heartily repent of.
He appeared to me as if he had been in great
trouble, as his countenance was very much altered.
I asked him what he had done ; he told me that
being bewitched to his acquaintance, he resolved to
proceed farther in the art, and to have a familiar
Spirit at his command, according to the directions
of his book ; which was to have book of what he
called Virgin's Parchment, consecrated with several
incantations ; as also a particular ink-horn, ink,
and pen ; with those he was to go out as usual to
a cross way, and call up a Spirit, and ask him his
name, which he was to put in the first page of

his book ; and this was to be his familiar Spirit.
Thus he was to do by as many as he pleased, writing their names in distinct pages, only one in a leaf ;
and then   whenever he took the book and opened it,
this Spirit whose name appeared should appear also.
The familiar Spirit he had, was called Malachi,
i. e. my King ;---an Hebrew name of an evil signification to him ; i. e. that an evil Spirit was become
his King.   After this they appeared faster than he
wished them, and in most dreadful shapes ;---like
Serpents, Lions, Bears, &c. hissing at him, and
attempting to throw spears and balls of fire upon
him, which did very much affright him ; and the
more so when he found it was not in his power to lay
them, expecting every moment to be torn to pieces.
This was in December, about mid-night, when he
continued there in great sweat, and from that
time he was never well so long as he lived. In the
course of his sickness, he often came to Mr.*****,
the Apothecary, in Broad-street, concerning a
cure ; but I know not whether he told him the ori-
ginal cause or not.   He also came to me at the
same time, and owned every matter as fact ; which
he had told before unto the last ; and insisted that
whenever he did any thing of that nature , he was
deluded in his conscience to think it lawful ; but
that he was since convinced to the contrary.   But
still asserted he made no compact with those Spirits,
never did harm to others by their means, nor ever
pryed into the future fortune of himself or others,

O

He expressed an hearty repentance for, and detestation of his sins ; so that though these matters cost him his life, yet I have room to believe him happy in the other world. I am not certain whether he gave this account to any other but myself, though he did relate something of it to Mr. Baily, Minister of St. James, in the City. Perhaps your Lordship may be farther informed by his relations and neighbours of *Mangots-field*, which is not above a mile out of the road to *Bath.* I have often told the story, but never mentioned his name before ; and therefore if your Lordship has a mind to print such accounts as these, I beg it might be with such tenderness to his memory as he deserved, and so as it may not be the least prejudice to his relations, who have the deserved character of an honest sober people. I am, with due respects,

Your Lordship's son, and servant,

ARTHUR BEDFORD."

Of the Devil's attempt to send out a Minister to preach the Gospel, &c.

The following very notable and interesting relation to young preachers, from the hand of the famous Minister of Christ Mr. Vavasor Powel, deserves a place in these accounts, which is as follows :---

"CONCERNING that delusion in *Kent*, (a relation of which I had, and still should have in the Country in writing, under the religious man's own hand, and some other brethren) though

I do not remember all the circumstances, yet the
substance of it was this-----There was one John
Moody, a religious man, under Bapt. (I suppose
first joyned Mr. Kyff, in *London*) Being in
bed one night, there appeared a great light in
his chamber, and a voice spoke to him thus ;
" John Moody, arise, and go to preach my gospel
" in the West, for my people perish for want of
" knowledge there."   To which John Moody
answered,   " I am not fit to preach, I want gifts."
The voice answered again, "I will give thee gifts,
" and fit thee."   Moody replyed, "I am a poor
" man, and have no means to maintain me therein."
The voice said, " Meet me at such a place (and
so named both time and place) and I will supply
thee with silver and gold," and so departed. The
next day, John Moody acquainted one or more
of his christian acquaintance ; and they fearing it
was a delusion, advised him to be very careful
what he did, and dissuaded him from going, coun-
selling him if it came again, he should ask who
he was, and particularly whether he was Jesus
of Nazareth, (for it was he that had power to send
out Ministers).   The Devil came again either the
next night or within a few nights after, in the same
manner, asking him why he did not go upon his
message ?   John Moody asked him who it was
that sent him ; the voice answered, I am God.
But saith he, art thou Jesus of Nazareth ? The
voice said again I am God.   Then John Moody

resolutely answered, if thou be not that Jesus that suffered at Jerusalem, and that sits at the right hand of God in heaven, I will not go. There-upon the Devil departed, making a great noise, and taking part of the top of the house away with him. This was the substance, and the thing undoubtedly true.

www.ingramcontent.com/pod-product-compliance
Lightning Source LLC
Chambersburg PA
CBHW030848090426
42737CB00009B/1149